INSIDE
ISLAM

Books by John Miller and Aaron Kenedi

God's Breath: Sacred Scriptures of the World

Muhammad Ali: Ringside

Revolution: Faces of Change

Life: A User's Manual

*Legends: Women Who Have Changed the World
Through the Eyes of Great Women Writers*

INSIDE
ISLAM

**THE FAITH, THE PEOPLE, AND THE CONFLICTS
OF THE WORLD'S FASTEST-GROWING RELIGION**

Edited by John Miller and Aaron Kenedi

Introduction by Akbar S. Ahmed

MARLOWE & COMPANY
NEW YORK

Compilation copyright © 2002 by John Miller and Aaron Kenedi
Introduction copyright © 2002 by Akbar S. Ahmed

Published by
Marlowe & Company
An Imprint of Avalon Publishing Group Incorporated
161 William Street, 16th Floor
New York, NY 10038

Editor's note: Changes for consistency have been made to the essays in this book.

Cover and interior design: Miller Design Partners
Cover photograph: Tim Hall/Getty Images
Permissions research: Shawneric Hachey
Proofreading and copyediting: Mimi Kusch

Library of Congress Control Number: 2002100740
ISBN 1-56924-568-1

9 8 7 6 5 4 3

Printed in the United States of America
Distributed by Publishers Group West

SPECIAL THANKS TO
AMY RENNERT
AND MATTHEW LORE

Contents

AKBAR S. AHMED

Introduction

THE TWENTY-FIRST CENTURY will be the century of Islam. Muslim civilization will be central to understanding where we will be moving in the future. Consider the facts: a population of 1.3 billion and growing; 55 states — and one of them nuclear; about 25 million living permanently in the West and many of them now making an impact on social, political, and economic life; and a religion that comes with commitment and passion.

Understanding Islam is therefore imperative to anyone wanting to make sense of living in the twenty-first century. Like many scholars in the field I have argued this point for the last two decades.

For anyone in doubt about the importance of understanding Islam, just switch on the television or read a newspaper. There is an Islamic story being reported from one or another part of the world at any given time. The fact that the hijackers of September 11, 2001, were Muslim meant that Islam

1

was now put under a microscope. Every kind of comment and theory was heard in the media from scholars to those who simply voiced their prejudices. Everyone seemed to have an opinion on Islam. And yet Islam was an unknown commodity to many in America.

Muhammad Ali, who has a capacity to convey a difficult idea with simple words, put it aptly to Oprah Winfrey: "Muslin is a piece of cloth, and Muslim is a person who belongs to the faith of Islam" (Oprah recounted this story when I was the expert guest on her show on Islam on October 5, 2001). If people could not even pronounce the name correctly, what hope was there for understanding the larger civilization, which is so complex, ancient, and sophisticated?

If we grant that Islam needs to be understood, the question then is how to begin. I suggest no better way than reading a volume like *Inside Islam*. The collection is a valuable contribution to the study of Islam. The editors have made wise choices: The contributors are well-known commentators, scholars, filmmakers, and, in the case of at least one of them, Nobel Prize winners.

As with all collections, there will be a debate and even controversy about who was selected and who was left out. Knowing something of the nature of the discussion around Islam, some Muslims will be unhappy with some of the contributors who they see as unduly critical of their religion. Others will view the more familiar contributors as sympathetic. I believe that by including both those who are perceived as overly critical and those who are sympathetic the editors of this volume have made the right choice.

Islam is a mosaic. Spread over the globe, with its societies speaking different languages, its peoples living in distinct political cultures, while aware of the unity of faith and vision that binds all Muslims, Islam can only be understood in its diversity.

The first part of the volume outlines the main features of the faith itself. We learn of the Holy Book and the Holy Prophet of Islam. We also are told of the significance of Mecca, where it all began for Muslims. The second part informs us of different Muslim people. We learn of Muslims in America, Iran, Malaysia, Indonesia, Egypt, Turkey, and Afghanistan. Here we come across Muslims living in the Arab heartland, in the Far East, and in the West. The final part of the volume raises contemporary issues that concern people looking at Islam. It is appropriately titled "The Conflicts." It contains the well-known essay by Bernard Lewis, "The Roots of Muslim Rage," which formed the conceptual base for Samuel Huntington's *Clash of Civilizations* published in 1993. The last essay in the volume, by Fareed Zakaria, attempts to answer the question so many Americans, including President George Bush, asked: "Why do they hate us?"

As the reader discovers Islam, he or she will not fail to notice that Islam is embedded in the Abrahamic tradition and shares the same religious message contained in Judaism and Christianity. Not only the idea of the one transcendent God, but even the great biblical names — Abraham, Moses, Jesus — are the same in Islam.

In spite of the similarities, many in the West think of Islam as the civilization most likely to clash with the West. September 11, 2001, confirmed this idea for many. However, it is also worth noting that there are many who believe in an idea opposed to that of the clash of civilizations, and that is the idea of the dialogue of civilizations. And it is worth pointing out that this idea was presented to the United Nations in 1998 by President Mohammed Khattami of Iran. Because his country is known as a land of extremism and fanaticism in the West, people were taken aback, but the idea of dialogue is central to Islam.

Indeed, Islam has much to contribute to this century. Islam's ideas of justice, compassion, and tolerance can contribute to a world desperately in need of these. It is here where Islam joins with those who desire a world based on these rules. However, for this vision to be fulfilled, Muslims and non-Muslims must work together in a spirit of mutual understanding. The first step is to begin to understand Islam.

DR. AKBAR S. AHMED

IBN KHALDUN CHAIR OF ISLAMIC
STUDIES AND PROFESSOR OF
INTERNATIONAL RELATIONS
SCHOOL OF INTERNATIONAL UNIVERSITY

AMERICAN UNIVERSITY
WASHINGTON, D.C.
JANUARY 2002

INSIDE
ISLAM

THE
FAITH

Islam

WE CAN BEGIN with an anomaly. Of all the non-Western religions, Islam stands closest to the West — closest geographically, and also closest ideologically; for religiously it stands in the Abrahamic family of religions, while philosophically it builds on the Greeks. Yet despite this mental and spatial proximity, Islam is the most difficult religion for the West to understand. "No part of the world," an American columnist has written, "is more hopelessly and systematically and stubbornly misunderstood by us than that complex of religion, culture and geography know as Islam."

This is ironic, but the irony is easily explained. Proximity is no

HUSTON SMITH *is a renowned world religions scholar and the author of numerous books on comparative religion. His classic* The World's Religions *has been an essential text since 1958. That book's section on Islam, excerpted here, is an insightful look at the history and principles of this unique religion.*

guarantee of concord — tragically, more homicides occur within families than anywhere else. Islam and the West are neighbors. Common borders have given rise to border disputes, which, beginning with raids and counter-raids, have escalated into vendettas, blood feuds, and all-out war. There is a happier side; in times and places Christians, Muslims, and Jews have lived together harmoniously — one thinks of Moorish Spain. But for a good part of the last fourteen hundred years, Islam and Europe have been at war, and people seldom have a fair picture of their enemies. . . .

Mistakes begin with its very name. Until recently it was called Muhammadanism by the West, which is not only inaccurate but offensive. It is inaccurate, Muslims say, because Muhammad didn't create this religion; God did — Muhammad was merely God's mouthpiece. Beyond this, the title is offensive because it conveys the impression that Islam focuses on a man rather than on God. To name Christianity after Christ is appropriate, they say, for Christians believe that Christ was God. But to call Islam Muhammadanism is like calling Christianity St. Paulism. The proper name of this religion is Islam. Derived from the root *s-l-m*, which means primarily "peace" but in a secondary sense "surrender," its full connotation is "the peace that comes when one's life is surrendered to God." This makes Islam — together with Buddhism, from *budh*, awakening-one of the two religions that is named after the attribute it seeks to cultivate; in Islam's case, life's total surrender to God. Those who adhere to Islam are known as Muslims.

"Around the name of the Arabs," writes Philip Hitti,

"gleams that halo which belongs to the world-conquerors. Within a century after their rise this people became the masters of an empire extending from the shores of the Atlantic Ocean to the confines of China, an empire greater than that of Rome at its zenith. In this period of unprecedented expansion, they assimilated to their creed, speech, and even physical type, more aliens that any stock before or since, not excepting the Hellenic, the Roman, the Anglo-Saxon, or the Russian."

Central in this Arab rise to greatness was their religion, Islam. If we ask how it came into being, the outsider's answer points to socio-religious currents that were playing over Arabia in Muhammad's day and uses them to explain what happened. The Muslim's answer is different. Islam begins not with Muhammad in sixth-century Arabia, they say, but with God. "In the beginning God . . ." the book of Genesis tells us. The Qur'an agrees. It differs only in using the word Allah. Allah is formed by joining the definite article *al* (meaning "the") with *ilah* (God). Not *a* god, for there is only one. Literally *Allah* means "*The* God." When the masculine plural, ending *im* is dropped from the Hebrew word for God, *Elohim*, the two words sound much alike.

God created the world, and after it human beings. The name of the first man was Adam. The descendants of Adam led to Noah, who had a son named Shem. This is where the word Semite comes from; literally a Semite is a descendant of Shem. Like the Jews, the Arabs consider themselves a Semitic people. The descendants of Shem led to Abraham, and so far we are still in the tradition of Judaism and Christianity.

Indeed, it was the submission of Abraham in his supreme test — would he be willing to sacrifice his son? — that appears to have provided Islam with its name. Abraham married Sarah. Sarah had no son, so Abraham, wanting to continue his line, took Hagar for his second wife. Hagar bore him a son, Ishmael, whereupon Sarah conceived and likewise had a son, named Isaac. Sarah then demanded that Abraham banish Ishmael and Hagar from the tribe. Here we come to the first divergence between the qur'anic and biblical accounts. According to the Qur'an, Ishmael went to the place where Mecca was to rise. His descendants, flourishing in Arabia, become Muslims; whereas those of Isaac, who remained in Palestine, were Hebrews and became Jews.

Following Ishmael's line in Arabia, we come in the latter half of the sixth century A.D. to Muhammad, the prophet through whom Islam reached its definitive from, Muslims believe. There had been authentic prophets of God before him, but he was their culmination; hence he is called "The Seal of the Prophets." No valid prophets will follow him.

The world into which Muhammad was born is described by subsequent Muslims in a single word: ignorant. Life under the conditions of the desert had never been serene. People felt almost no obligation to anyone outside their tribes. Scarcity of material goods made brigandage a regional institution and the proof of virility. In the sixth century political deadlock and the collapse of the magistrate in the leading city of Mecca aggravated this generally chaotic situation. Drunken orgies were commonplace, and the gaming impulse uncontrolled. The prevailing religion watched from the sidelines, providing

no check. Best described as an animistic polytheism, it peo-
pled the sandy wastes with beastly sprites called *jinn* or
demons. Fantastic personifications of desert terrors, they
inspired neither exalted sentiments nor moral restraint. Conditions could hardly have been better calculated to produce a
smoldering undercurrent, which erupted in sudden affrays
and blood feuds, some of which extended for half a century.
The times called for a deliverer.

He was born into the leading tribe of Mecca, the Kor-
eish, in approximately A.D. 570, and was named Muhammad, "highly praised," which name has since been borne by
more male children than any other in the world. His early
life was cradled in tragedy, for his father died a few days
before he was born, his mother when he was six, and his
grandfather, who cared for him after his mother's death,
when he was eight. Thereafter he was adopted into his
uncle's home. Though the latter's declining fortunes forced
the young orphan to work hard minding his uncle's flocks,
he was warmly received by his new family. The angels of
God, we are told, had opened Muhammad's heart and filled
it with light. . . .

A mountain on the outskirts of Mecca, known as Mount
Hira, contained a cave, and Muhammad, needing solitude,
began to frequent it. Peering into the mysteries of good and
evil, unable to accept the crudeness, superstition, and fratri-
cide that were accepted as normal, "this great fiery heart,
seething, simmering like a great furnace of thought," was
reaching out for God.

The desert *jinn* were irrelevant to this quest, but one deity was not. Named Allah, he was worshiped by the Meccans not as the only God but as an impressive one nonetheless. Creator, supreme provider, and determiner of human destiny, he was capable of inspiring authentic religious feeling and genuine devotion. Certain contemplatives of the time, called *hanifs*, worshiped Allah exclusively, and Muhammad was one of their number. Through vigils, often lasting the entire night, Allah's reality became for Muhammad increasingly evident and awesome. Fearful and wonderful, real as life, real as death, real as the universe he had ordained, Allah (Muhammad was convinced) was far greater than his countrymen supposed. This God, whose majesty overflowed a desert cave to fill all heaven and earth, was surely not a god or even the greatest of gods. He was what his name literally claimed: He was *the* God, One and only, One without rival. Soon from this mountain cave was to sound the greatest phrase of the Arabic language; the deep, electrifying cry that was to rally a people and explode their power to the limits of the known world: *a ilaha illa 'Llah!* There is no god but God!

But first the prophet must receive, around 610, his commission. Gradually, as Muhammad's visits to the cave became more compelling, the command that he later saw as predestined took form. It was the same command that had fallen earlier on Abraham, Moses, Samuel, Isaiah, and Jesus. Wherever, whenever, this call comes, its form may differ but its essence is the same. A voice falls from heaven saying, "You are the appointed one." On the Night of Power, as a strange peace pervaded creation and all nature was turned toward its Lord, in the middle of that night, say the Muslims, the Book was opened to a ready soul. Some add that on the anniversary of that Night it is possible to hear the grass grow and the trees speak, and that those who do so become saints or sages, for on the annual return of that Night one can see through the fingers of God.

On the first Night of Power, as Muhammad lay on the floor of the cave, his mind locked in deepest contemplation, there came to him an angel in the form of a man. The angel said to him: "Proclaim!" and he said: "I am not a proclaimer"; whereupon, as Muhammad was himself to report, "the Angel took me and whelmed me in his embrace until he had reached the limit of my endurance. Then he released me and said again, "Proclaim!" Again I said: "I am not a proclaimer," and again he whelmed me in his embrace. When again he had reached the limit of my endurance he said 'Proclaim!' and when I again protested, he whelmed me for a third time, this time saying:

Proclaim in the name of your Lord who created!
Created man from a clot of blood
Proclaim: Your Lord is the Most Generous,
Who teaches by the pen;
Teaches man what he know not.
(Qur'an 96:1–3)

Arousing from his trance, Muhammad felt as if the words he had heard had been branded on his soul. Terrified, he rushed home and fell into paroxysms. Coming to himself, he told Khadija that he had become either a prophet or "one possessed — mad." At first she resisted this disjunction, but on hearing his full story she became his first convert — which, Muslims often remark, in itself speaks well for his authenticity, for if anyone understands a man's true character it is his wife. "Rejoice, O dear husband, and be of good cheer," she said. "You will be the Prophet of this people."

We can imagine the spiritual anguish, the mental doubts, the waves of misgivings that followed in the wake of the experience. Was the voice really God's? Would it come again? Above all, what would it require?

It returned repeatedly, and its command was always the same — to proclaim. "O thou, inwrapped in thy mantle, arise and warn, and glorify the Lord." Muhammad's life was no more his own. From that time forth it was given to God and to humanity, preaching with unswerving purpose in the face of relentless persecution, insult, and outrage, the words that God was to transmit for twenty-three years. . . .

In an age charged with supernaturalism, when miracles were accepted as the stock-in-trade of the most ordinary saint, Muhammad refused to pander to human credulity. To miracle-hungry idolaters seeking signs and portents, he cut the issue clean: "God has not sent me to work wonders; He has sent me to preach to you. My Lord; be praised! Am I more than a man sent as an apostle?" From first to last he resisted every impulse to inflate his own image. "I never said that God's treasures are in my hand, that I knew the hidden things, or that I was an angel. I am only a preacher of God's words, the bringer of God's message to mankind." If signs be sought, let them be not of Muhammad's greatness but of

God's, and for these one need only open one's eyes. The heavenly bodies holding their swift, silent course in the vault of heaven, the incredible order of the universe, the rain that falls to relieve the parched earth, palms bending with golden fruit, ships that glide across the seas laden with goodness — can these be the handiwork of gods of stone? What fools to cry for signs when creation tokens nothing else! In an age of credulity, Muhammed taught respect for the world's incontrovertible order, a respect that was to bring Muslims to science before it did Christians. Apart from his nocturnal ascent through the heavens, which will be mentioned, he claimed only one miracle, that of the Qur'an itself. . . .

In *The 100: A Ranking of the Most Influential Persons in History*, Michael Hart places Muhammad first. His "unparalleled combination of secular and religious influence entitles Muhammad to be considered the most influential single figure in human history," Hart writes. The explanation that Muslims give for that verdict is simple. The entire work, they say, was the work of God.

The blend of admiration, respect, and affection that the Muslim feels for Muhammad is an impressive fact of history. They see him as a man who experienced life in exceptional range. Not only was he a shepherd, merchant, hermit, exile, soldier, lawmaker, prophet-priest-king, and mystic; he was also an orphan, for many years the husband of one wife much older than himself, a many times bereaved father, a widower, and finally the husband of many wives, some much younger than himself. In all of these roles he was exemplary. All this is in the minds of Muslims as they add to the mention of his name the benediction, "Blessings and peace be upon him." Even so, they never mistake him for the earthly center of their faith. That place is reserved for the bible of Islam, the Qur'an.

Literally, the work *al-qur'an* in Arabic (and hence "qur'an,") means a recitation. Fulfilling that purpose, the Qur'an is perhaps the most recited (as well as read) book in the world. Certainly, it is the world's most memorized book, and possibly the one that exerts the most influence on those who read it. So great was Muhammad's regard for its contents that (as we have seen) he considered it the only major miracle God worked through him — God's "standing miracle," as he called it. That he himself, unschooled to the extent that he was unlettered (*ummi*) and could barely write his name, could have produced a book that provides the ground plan of all knowledge and at the same time is grammatically perfect and without poetic peer — this, Muhammad, and with him all Muslims, are convinced defies belief. He put the point in a rhetorical question: "Do you ask for a greater miracle than this, O unbelieving people, than to have your language chosen as the language of that incomparable Book, one piece of which puts all your golden poetry to shame?"

Four-fifths the length of the New Testament, the Qur'an is divided into 114 chapters or *surahs*, which (with the exception of the short first chapter that figures in the Muslim's daily prayer) are arranged in order of decreasing length. Thus Surah Two has 286 verses, Surah Three has two hundred, down to Surah 114, which has only six.

Muslims tend to read the Qur'an literally. They consider

it the earthly facsimile of an Uncreated Qur'an in almost exactly the way that Christians consider Jesus to have been the human incarnation of God. The comparison that reads, "If Christ is God incarnate, the Qur'an is God Inlibriate" (from *liber*, Latin for book) is inelegant but not inaccurate. The created Qur'an is the instantiation, in letters and sounds, of the Qur'an's limitless essence in its Uncreated Form. Not that there are two Qur'ans, of course. Rather, the created Qur'an is the formal crystallization of the infinite reality of the Uncreated Qur'an. Two levels of reality are operative here. There is the Divine Reality of the Uncreated Qur'an, and there is the earthly reality of the created Qur'an. When the created Qur'an is said to be a miracle, the miracle referred to is the presence of the Uncreated Qur'an within the letters and sounds of its created (and therefore necessarily in certain ways circumscribed) manifestation.

The words of the Qur'an came to Muhammad in manageable segments over twenty-three years through voices that seemed at first to vary and sometimes sounded like "the reverberating of bells," but which gradually condensed into a single voice that identified itself as Gabriel's. Muhammad had no control over the flow of the revelation; it descended on him independent of his will. When it arrived he was changed into a special state that was externally discernible. Both his appearance and the sound of his voice would change. He reported that the words assaulted him as if they were solid and heavy: "For We shall charge thee with a word of weight" (73:5; all such references in this chapter are to *surah* and verse[s] in the Qur'an). Once they descended while he was riding a camel. The animal sought vainly to support the added weight by adjusting its legs. By the time the revelation ceased, its belly was pressed against the earth and its legs splayed out. The words that Muhammad exclaimed in these often trance-like states were memorized by his followers and recorded on bones, bark, leaves, and scraps of parchment, with God preserving their accuracy throughout.

The Qur'an continues the Old and new Testament, God's earlier revelations, and presents itself as their culmination: "We made a covenant of old with the Children of Israel [and] you have nothing of guidance until you observe the Torah and the Gospel" (5:70, 68). This entitles Jews and Christians to be included with Muslims as "People of the Book." (Because the context of the qur'anic revelation is the Middle East, religions of other lands are not mentioned, but their existence is implied and in principle validated, as in the following verses: "To every people we have sent a messenger. . . . [Some] We have mentioned to you, and [some] we have not mentioned to you" [10:47, 4:164]). Nevertheless, Muslims regard the Old and New Testaments as sharing two defects from which the Qur'an is free. For circumstantial reasons they record only portions of Truth. Second, the Jewish and Christian Bibles were partially corrupted in transmission, a fact that explains the occasional discrepancies that occur between their accounts and parallel ones in the Qur'an. Exemption from these two limitations makes the Qur'an the final and infallible revelation of God's will. Its second chapter says explicitly: "This is the Scripture whereof there is no doubt."

From the outside things look otherwise, for from without the Qur'an is all but impenetrable. No one has ever curled up on a rainy weekend to read the Qur'an. Carlyle confessed that it was "as toilsome reading as I ever undertook; a wearisome, confused jumble, crude, incondite. Nothing but a sense of duty could carry any European through the Qur'an." Sir Edward Gibbon said much the same: "The European will peruse with impatience its endless incoherent rhapsody of fable and precept, and declamation, which seldom excites sentiment or an idea, which sometimes crawls in the dust, and is sometimes lost in the clouds." How are we to understand the discrepancy of the Qur'an as read from within and from without?

The language in which it was proclaimed, Arabic, provides an initial clue. "No people in the world," writes Philip Hitti "are so moved by the word, spoken or written, as the Arabs. Hardly any language seems capable of exercising over the minds of its users such irresistible influence as Arabic." Crowds in Cairo, Damascus, or Baghdad can be stirred to the highest emotional pitch by statements that, when translated, seem banal. The rhythm, melodic cadence, the rhyme produce a powerful hypnotic effect. Thus the power of the qur'anic revelation lies not only in the literal meaning of its words but also in the language in which this meaning incorporated, including its sound. The Qur'an was from the first a vocal phenomenon; we remember that we are to "recite" in the name of the Lord! Because content and container are here inseparably fused, translations cannot possibly convey the emotion, the fervor, and the mystery that the Qur'an holds in the original. This is why, in sharp contrast to Christians, who have translated their Bible into every known script, Muslims have preferred to teach others the language in which they believe God spoke finally with incomparable force and directness. It is impossible to overemphasize the central position of the Qur'an in the elaboration of any Islamic doctrine. With large portions memorized in childhood, it regulates the interpretation and evaluation of every event. It is a memorandum for the faithful, a reminder for daily doings, and a repository of revealed truth. It is a manual of definitions and guarantees, and at the same time a road map for the will. Finally, it is a collection of maxims to meditate on in private, deepening endlessly one's sense of the divine glory. "Perfect is the Word of you Lord in truth and justice" (6:115). . . .

For long periods since Muhammad called his people to God's oneness, Muslims have wandered from the spirit of the Prophet. Their leaders are the first to admit that practice has often been replaced by mere profession, and that fervor has waned.

Viewed as a whole, however, Islam unrolls before us one of the most remarkable panoramas in all history. We have spoken of its early greatness. Had we pursued its history there would have been sections on the Muslim empire, which, a century after Muhhamad's death, stretched from the bay of Biscay to the Indus and the frontiers of China, from the Aral Sea to the upper Nile. More important would have been the sections describing the spread of Muslim ideas: the development of a fabulous culture, the rise of liter-

ature, science, medicine, art, and architecture; the glory of
Damascus, Baghdad, and Egypt, and the splendor of Spain
under the Moors. There would have been the story of how,
during Europe's Dark Ages, Muslim philosophers and
scientists kept the lamp of learning bright, ready to spark the
Western mind when it roused from its long sleep.

Nor would the story have been entirely confined to the
past, for there are indications that Islam is emerging from
several centuries of stagnation, which colonization no doubt
exacerbated. It faces enormous problems: how to distinguish
industrial modernization (which on balance it welcomes)
from Westernization (which on balance it doesn't); how to
realize the unity that is latent in Islam when the forces of
nationalism work powerfully against it; how to hold on to
Truth in a pluralistic, relativizing age. But having thrown off
the colonial yoke, Islam is stirring with some of the vigor
of its former youth. From Morocco across from Gibraltar
on the Atlantic, eastward across North Africa, through
the Indian subcontinent (which includes Pakistan and
Bangladesh), on to the near-tip of Indonesia, Islam is a vital
force in the contemporary world. Numbering in the order of
900 million adherents in a global population of 5 billion, one
person out of every five or six belongs today to this religion
which guides human thought and practice in unparalleled
detail. And the proportion is increasing. Read these words at
any hour of day or night and somewhere from a minaret (or
now by radio) a *muezzin* will be calling the faithful to prayer,
announcing:

God is most great
God is most great.
I testify that there is no god but God.
I testify that Muhammad is the Prophet of God.
arise and pray;
God is most great.
God is most great.
There is no god but God.

AKBAR S. AHMED

Muhammad

O UNDERSTAND ISLAM, it is crucial to understand the nature of its Prophet and holy book, the Qur'an. For that it is necessary to journey to what is now Saudi Arabia.

A few miles from Makkah (Mecca) is a bleak and forbidding mountain called Hira which rises abruptly from the earth. It has a steep and jagged face pointing toward Makkah. On top, precariously perched, is a cave. It was here that one of the most remarkable events of history took place in the seventh century. The event centered on Muhammad ibn Abdullah (son of Abdullah), who was in the habit of retreating to Hira to meditate during the month of Ramadan. In A.D. 610, when he was aged about forty, he heard the voice of the angel

AKBAR S. AHMED *is the chair of Islamic Studies at American University. He is a respected academic and the author of numerous books on Islam, including* Discovering Islam. *This biography of Islam's central figure, the prophet Muhammad, is taken from his 1999 book,* Islam Today.

Gabriel. It ordered him to recite some of the divine verses of the Qur'an. The Qur'an was thus revealed; the world would henceforth know Muhammad as the Prophet of Islam. (Whenever Muslims speak or write the Prophet's name, they usually add, "May the peace and blessing of Allah be upon him," sometimes written as "pbuh," short for "peace be upon him," or its Arabic translation "salla Allaju Alayhi wasallam," which is abbreviated to "saw." Many even make a gesture of kissing their fingers and touching them to their eyes and lips as a further sign of respect.)

The Prophet's retreat to Hira — known as "the mountain of light" after the revelations — tells us many interesting things about him. It confirms for us his contemplative nature and his desire to search for answers to the eternal problems that face human beings. It suggests a man prepared to undergo sacrifice and physical hardship in his quest (Hira is a formidable climb; and the Prophet was no longer a young man when he used to go there). It also echoes a pattern established by the earlier prophetic figures — Jesus, Moses, Abraham — who retreated from the hurly-burly of the world to caves and mountains for spiritual renewal.

As the Prophet is central to the understanding of Islam, many question relating to him are raised. What sort of a man was he? What kind of society did he live in? What was his message? What impact did it have on history? And how is it relevant to us in our times?

The Prophet's Early Life

MORE THAN ANY EARLIER religious figure — such as Jesus, Moses, or Abraham — the Prophet lived his life in the full glare of history. He is neither a mythological nor a semi-divine figure but lived like other people. His triumphs, joys, pain, sorrow, and anger are documented. His gentleness, compassion, piety — his "humanness" — would help explain why for Muslims he is simply *insan-i-kamil*, the perfect person. But his human nature would allow critics to mock him.

The Prophet belonged to the Banu Hashim (sons of Hashim), one of the clans of the powerful Quraish tribe that dominated Makkah, the chief trading center on the Arabian peninsula. It was a vast land, one million square miles in size, consisting largely of deserts and mountains, where nomadic and pastoral Bedouin tribes led a precarious existence. Their social habits reflected the ecology which, in a sociological sense, helped to form them. The extended family or clan was at the core of society. Several clans formed a tribe. Each tribe was led by a chief who was *primus inter pares*, first among equals. He was usually selected by a consensus among his peers. The tribal code permeated society.

In the time of the Prophet's youth, religion meant numerous gods and goddesses, often worshiped through trees and stones. While the tribal code encouraged the notion of *muruwwa*, manhood, which was glorification of tribal chivalry, the treatment of women was abominable. Female infanticide was common. Society was on the verge of anarchy and disorder. This period before the coming of Islam would be known subsequently as *Jahiliyya,* or the age of ignorance.

The Prophet was born about the year A.D. 570 in Makkah. His father had died a few weeks earlier. Since it was the custom for newborn babies to be fed by a foster-mother, at first the Prophet was cared for by a Bedouin woman, Halimah. This relationship has ensured a special place for Halimah in Muslim affection and folklore.

The Prophet's mother died when he was six and he went to live with his grandfather, Abdul Muttalib. Just two years later his grandfather also died, and he was then cared for by his uncle, Abu Talib, a merchant. The sense of loss at such an early age made him a pensive and sensitive person. He would always emphasize the need to be especially kind to orphans, women, the weak in society. As a boy, he looked after sheep in the desert. Later he would look back with quiet satisfaction. "Allah," he would say, 'sent no prophet who was not a shepherd.'

An incident in his early life reveals his manner of dealing with disputes. Pilgrims gathered in Makkah to marvel at the black stone that was kept in the Kabah, the designated holy site which was guarded by the Quraish. The Arabs believed the black stone came from heaven and was a divine sign. After the coming of Islam, the Kabah, which is a simple cube-shaped building now covered with black and gold cloth, would be regarded by Muslims as God's first house on earth, built by Adam and later rebuilt by the prophet Abraham and his son Ismail. But during the time when the Arabs were pagans the Kabah housed hundreds of idols.

One year, heavy rain had damaged the walls of the Kabah.

Extensive repairs were needed, and the four major tribes of Makkah were to share the work. The work proceeded without a hitch until the time came to replace the black stone. Then an argument began which reflected typical tribal society and its notions of esteem. Which tribe would have the honor of actually putting the stone in place?

If the matter was not resolved amicably it could start a tribal war. To prevent this from happening an old man made a suggestion. They would let the gods help: The first person to walk through the temple gates next day would be asked to solve the dispute. The first person turned out to be the Prophet. While still a young man the Prophet was well known and respected for his honesty — he was widely called *al-Amin*, "the honest one." His solution to the dispute was simple. Taking a cloak, he spread it on the ground. The black stone was placed on it and leaders from each tribe took hold of the four corners of the cloak. Holding tight, they lifted the stone and then the Prophet slid it into place.

The Prophet's Marriage

AMONG THE QURAISH there was a respected and wealthy widow named Khadijah, who was involved in trade. On hearing of the Prophet's reputation, she sent for him and asked him to take her goods and trade them in Syria. He agreed, and left for Syria with one of Khadijah's caravans. Accompanying the caravan was Khadijah's slave, Maysarah.

Long journeys are when you get to know your companions; nothing can be hidden for long. So as Maysarah came to know the Prophet he grew to admire him. He was not like any other man he had met.

Two events took place during this journey which greatly puzzled Maysarah and are now part of history, recounted by millions of Muslims. The first happened when the caravan stopped for a break near the lonely home of Bahira, a Christian monk. The Prophet sat under a tree while Maysarah was busy with some work. The monk came up to Maysarah and asked, "Who is the man resting under the tree?" "One of the Quraish, the people who guard the Kabah," replied Maysarah. The monk shook his head in wonder, saying, "No one but a Prophet is sitting beneath this tree."

The second event occurred on the return journey. As they crossed the desert, Maysarah, who was riding behind the Prophet, felt the heat of noon, and when the sun was at its hottest he saw two angels appear above the Prophet and shield him from the sun's harmful rays.

On their return Maysarah told Khadijah everything about the trip, including his observations about the Prophet's character and behavior. The trip was declared a success: The Prophet had made more profit for Khadijah than she had ever received before.

Khadijah was intrigued. Wealthy and attractive, she had declined many marriage offers. Now she was interested. She sent a friend to ask the Prophet why he was not married. The reply was that he had no money to support a family. The friend then asked: "Supposing a rich, beautiful, and noble lady agreed to marry you?" The Prophet was curious about her identity. The friend told him it was Khadijah. He went with his uncles, Abu Talib and Hamzah, to see Khadijah's uncle, and asked his permission to marry her. The uncle agreed and soon after the Prophet and Khadijah were married.

Although there was an age difference (Khadijah was some fifteen years older), the marriage was a happy one and they were well suited to each other. Khadijah would play a critical role in the coming of Islam, standing like a pillar beside her husband when the first revelations came; indeed she would have the singular honor of being the first Muslim in history.

They had six children, two sons and four daughters. There was domestic sorrow: their first-born, a son called Qasim, died shortly before his second birthday, and their last child, also a son, lived only a short time. But their four daughters — Zainab, Ruqayyah, Umm Kalthum, and Fatimah — all survived, and played important roles in Islamic history.

The First Words of the Message

THE MESSAGE OF ISLAM was first revealed to the Prophet in 610, when he was engaged in one of his periods of retreat to the cave on Hira. One night, during the month of Ramadan, an angel appeared to him. "Read," he said. But the Prophet was unlettered and could neither read nor write. Three times the Prophet said he could not read and three times the angel insisted. It was as if someone was squeezing his heart. Then the angel taught him this verse:

Read in the name of thy Lord who created,
Created man, out of a clot of congealed blood.

Read! And they lord is most Bountiful,
He who taught (the use of) the Pen,
Taught man that which he knew not.
(The Qur'an, *surah* 96: verses 1–5)

When he returned home he was assailed by many questions and emotions. But Khadijah had little doubt that something very special was happening in their lives. One of her
Christian relatives, the saintly priest Waraqah, explained to
the Prophet that he had seen God's messenger, the angel
Gabriel. Khadijah reassured him that it was a sign that he
had been chosen as a prophet. A short while later, he had
another vision of the angel Gabriel on Hira. This frightened
him and he came hurrying home. Once again, Khadijah was
a rock of comfort. It now dawned on him: God had chosen
him for a special purpose, as the Messenger.

After those momentous revelations in the month of
Ramadan, others came regularly to the Prophet. Islam was
now proclaimed to the world (the word itself means submission to the will of God). The Prophet knew what he had to
do and prepared himself for what was to come. Khadijah was
the first to accept Islam. Then one day the Prophet's young
cousin, Ali, found the Prophet and Khadijah praying. He
was curious and asked what they were doing. The Prophet
explained the nature of Islam. That night Ali could not sleep.
He was thinking about what the Prophet had said. He had
great admiration and respect for his cousin and his words had
made a deep impression. By dawn he had come to a decision:
He too would accept Islam. Thus, as Khadijah is the first

female to embrace Islam, Ali is the first male.

Now the Prophet began to preach Islam openly; but few people took him seriously. The Quraish were increasingly hostile. They had good reason. The idols of Makkah which symbolized degradation and ignorance had become the focus of the Prophet's preaching. When the Prophet told them not to pray to these idols the people of Makkah were furious. Pilgrims came to visit their pagan shrines and brought business. The Prophet's talk would destroy it; the merchants were outraged. So they called him a liar and a madman. Some of the early Muslims were beaten up and tortured. The attacks grew worse.

What the Quraish did made no impression on the Prophet. He would to not be deterred from spreading his message. When the Quraish offered him a blank check — untold wealth, leadership, anything — if he gave up his ideas, he replied: "I would not do so — even if you placed the sun in my right hand and the moon in my left hand."

The Journey Across the Desert: The Hijra

HOWEVER, A CRISIS POINT was approaching. There was talk of assassination, and plots were being hatched. At this stage, pilgrims from the city of Yathrib — or Madinah — heard the Prophet preach and were impressed. They invited him to come and live with them, over four hundred kilometers away across the Arabian desert, and the Prophet accepted their invitation.

The journey in 622 across the desert is a crucial event for Muslims. It is called the *hijra*, which means departure. Even today, the Muslim system of dating years starts with the Prophet's journey; A.D. 622 is the first year of the Muslim calendar. On another level, the *hijra* suggests that Muslims must not live under tyranny, that they must remake their lives elsewhere if necessary in order to practice their faith. So deep would be the Prophet's attachment to Madinah that he would be buried there, thus providing the second most holy place for Muslims after the Kabah in Makkah.

In Madinah, the Prophet started the first Muslim community. Rules and regulations which govern a society were formulated and these still influence Muslims today. The first mosque was built next to the Prophet's house. The Prophet himself helped to build the mosque. He taught that everyone was equal in the eyes of God. "None of you can be a believer unless he loves for his brother what he loves for himself," said the Prophet. To set an example he mended his own clothes and did his own shopping. The Prophet's compassion extended to all creation, not just human beings. After all the Qur'an has said: "No creature is there crawling on the earth, no bird flying with its wings, but they are nations like yourselves" (*surah* 6: verse 38).

Many stories are told of the Prophet's humility and kindness. Here is one example. Abu Hurayrah went to the market with the Prophet to buy some clothes. The seller stood up and kissed the hand of the Prophet. The Prophet withdrew his hand and stopped the man from kissing his hand, saying, "This is the practice of the Persians with their kings. I am not a king. I am only a man from among you." The garments were purchased and Abu Hurayrah wanted to carry them for the Prophet. The Prophet did not allow him and said: "The owner of something has more right to carry it."

So great is the respect and affection the Prophet commands that his very sayings, *hadith*, are the source of wisdom and social practice in the Muslim world. These cover the entire range of human activity. Since there was always the danger of people incorrectly attributing things to the Prophet, scholars collected and authenticated "genuine" *hadith*. Intensive research was involved as each hadith was rejected or accepted depending on it traceable links to the Prophet. The integrity of those who formed the links needed to be unimpeachable. Thus each *hadith* required a chain of those who had actually heard the saying and could trace it to the Prophet. The exercise is an Islamic science. Centuries ago Imam Bukhari, who is generally considered the authority, selected about 7,300 from six hundred thousand in ninety-seven books.

Respect for the Prophet is reflected in the high status his descendants have always enjoyed. Called Sayyeds or Sharif or Shah, they are expected to behave with dignity and decorum. Although some who claim to be the Prophet's descendants have little evidence of their ancestry, many support their claims with genealogical charters.

The Later Marriages of the Prophet

THE PROPHET'S MARRIAGES have led to colorful innuendoes by critics of Islam. They were often cited in the Middle Ages to prove the voluptuous sensuality of the Prophet. In medieval Europe they helped create a powerful image which contrasted with the spiritual and ascetic Jesus, who never married. But even a cursory examination of the marriages will dispel the charge. The Prophet married Khadijah, older as we know by fifteen years, and led a happily monogamous life by all accounts until her death in 619. There are no hints of improper behavior during this period.

Once Islam spread, the war produced many widows. They would come to the Prophet in desperate straits. Many were daughters or wives of close companions. Sauda, the first wife he married after Khadijah's death, was a widow of forty, and one of the Muslims who had migrated to Abyssinia to escape persecution. She had a son by her previous husband. Rather than leave Sauda and her son destitute to fend for themselves in a society still used to treating women with cruelty, the Prophet asked her to share his home in honorable marriage.

The Prophet contracted twelve marriages in all after Khadijah. Most of his wives were between forty and fifty, divorced, often more than once, and had offspring by previous spouses when the Prophet married them. In the harsh terrain of Arabia, and in the difficult circumstances of those days, people aged rapidly, and these women would have been elderly. If the Prophet had wished for sensual pleasure there would have been no dearth of any kind of women available to him.

The marriages provided the women with pious and sheltered lives in the simple household of the Prophet. It is the Prophet's treatment of his wives — with fairness, gentleness and respect — that has laid the basis for the treatment of women in Islam. It must be understood that these marriages were only allowed to the Prophet. A Muslim is encouraged to marry once only but in extraordinary circumstances he may marry up to four wives.

If there had been sensuality or depravity in the Prophet's household the women themselves would have talked — as they often did, commenting critically on his austerity and attempts to be scrupulously fair between them. But they did not. On the contrary he inspired deep love in them, as the following story illustrates.

The Prophet is lying ill on his death-bed. His family and friends are around him, all deeply concerned. His beloved daughter, Fatimah, does not leave his bedside; she is dignified in her grief. He beckons to her and whispers in her ear. She begins to cry. A little while later he again says something to her. This time she smiles. Later, those close to her would ask the meaning of what transpired between father and daughter. "I cried," she said, "because my father said he did not have much time to live. But then he told me I would follow him soon. I was happy, as I would be with him again." This story is widely known among Muslims. It reveals the deep affection between a father and daughter. On another level it reflects on the brevity of life, the concept of death, its inevitability as part of the natural cycle of life, and the need to put it into perspective. The story also points to the idea of an afterlife. Above all, it shows the love that the man in the story inspired.

The Prophet's Last Address

THE PROPHET'S LAST ADDRESS at Arafat on his final pilgrimage, just before his death in 632, sums up the essence of Islam, It clearly identifies the five pillars upon which to rest Islamic belief and practice.

> O people, indeed your lives, your properties, and your honor are sacred and inviolable to you till you appear before your Lord. O people! Be conscious of God. And even if a mangled Abyssinian slave becomes your leader hearken to him and obey him as long as he establishes and institutes the Book of God.
>
> Worship your Lord and Sustainer. Perform your five daily *salat* [prayers]. Fast your month [of Ramadan]. Make pilgrimage to your House [the Kabah and Makkah]. Pay the *zakat* on your property willingly and obey whatever I command you. Then you will enter the Paradise of your Lord and Sustainer.

The address ends with the clearest statement possible of equality, of the need to abolish barriers created by race and colour. It is a message of the greatest relevance to our world with its ethnic and racial prejudices:

> All of you descend from Adam and Adam was made of earth. There is no superiority for an Arab over a non-Arab nor for a non-Arab over an Arab, neither for a white man over a black man nor a black man over a white man except the superiority gained through consciousness of God [*taqwa*]. Indeed the nobles among you is the one who is most deeply conscious of God.

THOMAS CLEARY

The Qur'an

THE QUR'AN IS undeniably a book of
great importance even to the non-Muslim,
perhaps more today than ever, if that is possible. One aspect of Islam that is unexpected and yet appealing to the post-Christian
secular mind is the harmonious interplay of faith and reason.
Islam does not demand unreasoned belief. Rather, it invites
intelligent faith, growing from observation, reflection, and
contemplation, beginning with nature and what is all around
us. Accordingly, antagonism between religion and science
such as that familiar to Western-
ers is foreign to Islam.

This connection between faith
and reason enabled Islamic civilization to absorb and vivify useful knowledge, including that of
ancient peoples, whereby it eventually nursed Europe out of the

THOMAS CLEARY 's
1993 translation of the
Qur'an is considered
by many to be the
definitive version.
The introduction,
excerpted here, reveals
why this holy book
is so important to the
Muslim faith.

Dark Ages, laying the foundation for the Renaissance. When Europe got on its cultural feet and expelled Islam, however, the European mind was rent by the inability of the Christian Church to tolerate the indivisibility of the sacred and the secular that characterized Islam and had enabled Islamic civilization to develop natural science and abstract art as well as philosophy and social science. The result was a painful, ill-fated divorce between science and religion in Europe, one whose consequences have adversely affected the entire world.

In the post-Christian West, where thinking people, including scientists themselves once more, are seeking solutions to the difficulties created by the Christian divorce between religion and science, the Qur'an offers a way to explore an attitude that fully embraces the quest for knowledge and understanding that is the essence of science, while at the same time, and indeed for the same reasons, fully embraces the awe, humility, reverence, and conscience without which "humankind does indeed go too far in considering itself to be self-sufficient" (Qur'an 96:6–7).

Even for the secular Westerner, apart from any question of religious belief or faith, there are immediate benefits to be found in reading the Qur'an. First, in view of the sacredness and vital importance of the Qur'an to approximately one-fifth of all humanity, a thinking citizen of the world can hardly develop a rational and mature social consciousness without considering the message of the Qur'an and its meaning for the Muslim community.

With the fall of communism, it has become particularly

clear that global peace, order, and self-determination of peoples cannot be achieved without intelligent respect for Islam and the inalienable right of Muslims to live their religion. The second immediate benefit in reading the Qur'an, therefore, is that it is a necessary step toward the understanding and tolerance without which world peace is in fact inconceivable.

For non-Muslims, one special advantage in reading the Qur'an is that it provides an authentic point of reference from which to examine the biased stereotypes of Islam to which Westerners are habitually exposed. Primary information is essential to distinguish between opinion and fact in a reasonable manner. This exercise may also enable the thinking individual to understand the inherently defective nature of prejudice itself, and thus be the more generally receptive to all information and knowledge of possible use to humankind.

The name Qur'an means the Recital or the Reading. According to its own word, the Qur'an is a revealed Book in the spiritual tradition of the Torah and Gospel transmitted by Moses and Jesus. Connecting itself and these distinguished predecessors to even earlier dispensations of original religion, the Qur'an represents its teaching as confirming and clarifying the truth of what was in those messages.

The Qur'an is undeniably unique in this tradition, and indeed unique in the entire context of classical sacred tradition throughout the world, in having been revealed in the full light of history, through the offices of a Prophet who was well known.

As the last link in a chain of revelation going back to time immemorial, even to the very origin of humankind, the Qur'an has the special function of recollecting the essential message of all revealed Books and distinguishing this from the opinions and reactions later interpolated into ancient texts whose original dispensation had taken place in remote and even unknown times.

Therefore the Qur'an is not only called the Reading or the Recital but also the Criterion: It is called a Reminder and also a Clarification. A modern descendant of the Prophet Muhammad wrote of this comprehensive scope and function of the Book in these terms:

> The Qur'an is nothing but the old books refined of human alloy, and contains transcendent truths embodied in all sacred scriptures with complete additions, necessary for the development of all human faculties. It repeats truths given in the Holy Vedas, in the Bible, in the words of the Gita, in the sayings of Buddha and all other prophets, and adds what was not in them, and gives new laws to meet the contingencies of the present time when the different members of God's family who lived apart from each other in the days of old revelations had come close one to the other.

Because the Qur'an synthesizes and perfects earlier revelations, its function as a Criterion to distinguish between truth and falsehood is not carried out in the form of dogmatic assertion or condemnation of one religion or another, but in the form of distinction between human artifice and the essential meaning of religion, between hypocrisy and true faith. Thus the same writer explains, "The Qur'an calls itself Hakam — 'judge,' to decide between Christian and Christian, between Hindu and Hindu, between Buddhist and Buddhist, and so it did." The observation that the Qur'an distinguishes the differences within the adherents of each religious dispensation, rather than among the dispensations themselves per se, seems to be a key to approaching the Qur'an without religious bias.

The Qur'an could not function in this manner in the context of world religions if it were no more than a collection of dogma or the handbook of a particular new sect or cult. The Qur'an speaks to humanity as a whole, to nations, communities, families, and individuals; complete with both an outer teaching and an inner teaching, it speaks both to persons and to souls, individually and collectively. A contemporary descendant of the Prophet writes of the often unsuspected depth, richness, and intrinsic breadth of the Qur'an in these terms:

> For Sufis of the classical period, the Qur'an is the encoded document which contains Sufi teachings. Theologians tend to assume that it is capable of interpretation only in a conventionally religious way; historians are inclined to look for earlier literary or religious sources; others for evidence of contemporary events reflected in its pages. For the Sufi, the Qur'an is a document with numerous levels of trans-

mission, each one of which has a meaning in accordance with the capacity for understanding of the reader. It is this attitude toward the book which made possible the understanding between people who were of nominally Christian, pagan, or Jewish backgrounds — a feeling which the orthodox could not understand. The Qur'an in one sense is therefore a document of psychological importance.

Here again it can be seen that the very least advantage we can derive from reading the Qur'an is the opportunity to examine our own subjectivity in understanding a text of this nature. This can have important educational consequences, both immediate and long-term, that can hardly be derived simply by imbibing received opinions and attitudes without individual thought and reflection.

As is well known, the Qur'an was revealed through the Prophet Muhammad, who was born around the year 570 C.E. Muhammad was of the noble Quraish clan, the custodians of the sacred shrine of Mecca, believed to have been built by Abraham in the remote past.

Orphaned at an early age, Muhammad developed into a sober and responsible young man, known for his trustworthiness. When he was twenty-five years old, he married his employer, a successful businesswoman most impressed by Muhammad's goodness.

The first revelation came when Muhammad was forty years old, a mature man of impeccable character. It took place during one of his periodic meditation retreats in a mountain cave outside Mecca. Far from inflated by the experience, Muhammad was fearful and demurred; he rushed home to his wife and anxiously revealed what had happened to him. Reminding him of his well-known virtues, she assured him that he was not mad. Then she took him to a cousin, a Christian, who listened to the beginnings of the Recital and declared it to be of the same Truth as that brought by Moses and Jesus.

The first Muslims were members of Muhammad's house. Beside his wife Khadijaha, there were the freed slave Zaid and Muhammad's young cousin and future son-in-law Ali. Shortly thereafter Abu Bakr, a longtime friend of Muhammad, also joined the fledgling community of Islam.

After a brief pause, revelations continued, and word of the new Muslim movement soon began to get around. This annoyed the leaders of the Quraish because they felt Islam undermined their authority. Teaching that there can by nature only be one real God, Islam undermined the religious authority of the Quraish as leaders of the old tribal polytheism. Attracting many converts from among slaves and other disenfranchised people, Islam was also seen to undermine the political authority of the dominant clan fathers. Preaching a level of humanness and social responsibility well above that realized by existing practices, Islam was also seen to diminish the moral stature of the tribal patriarchs.

For ten years Muhammad and the Muslims of Mecca were subjected to abuse and torture. A group of Muslims emigrated to Abyssinia, assured by the Prophet that the king of that land was Christian and would protect them. Eventually the leaders of the Quraish tried to assassinate Muhammad, and so the Prophet was finally forced to flee from Mecca in 622 C.E. This became known as the Year of the Emigration, the year from which all dates in Islamic history are counted.

The persecuted Muslims migrated en masse to Yathrib, later known as Medina al Nabiy, "The City of the Prophet," or simply as Medina, "The City." Hostilities and intrigues against them expanded, however, as the evident moral force of the movement aroused the hopes and fears of increasing numbers of individuals and groups. As a result, during nearly a decade of residence in Medina, Muhammad was repeatedly obliged to lead the Muslims in war. In one battle the Prophet was severely wounded in the head and face, and presumed dead.

At length Muhammad and the Muslims emerged triumphant, not by virtue of a crushing military victory but by constant devotion to Islam and indefatigable resistance to oppression. Poorly armed Muslims would face, and sometimes even defeat, battalions of trained warriors outnumbering them ten to one. And the movement continued to grow, in spite of opposition and hardships.

In the seventh year of the Emigration, Muhammad made the pilgrimage to Mecca, and in the next year the Prophet entered Mecca with a large party of Muslims, unopposed. He cleared the sacred shrine of idols and established worship of the one real God, including the practices of prayer, charity, and fasting. Through the promulgation of the Qur'an and his own example as an inspired Prophet, Muhammad also reformed many aspects of family, social, and economic life.

MICHAEL WOLFE

Mecca

MARRAKESH, MOROCCO. May 1, 1990. The lunar year rolled backward as the warm weather came on. Now that Ramadan was finished, the Hajj, the other engine of the Muslim calendar, began turning over. The rite would not take place until July, but a pilgrimage required preparation. The three-thousand-mile journey from Morocco to Saudi Arabia involved visas, reservations, and other arrangements. For many, these plans were already afoot, and the Hajj was becoming a topic in the medina. Every week the local papers carried more full-page advertisements for flights to Mecca. I began to meet a few pilgrims in the souk. They all were merchants.

Abdal-Hadi ran an electronics shop a few blocks from the Ben

MICHAEL WOLFE *'s 2000 book,* One Thousand Roads to Mecca, *profiles travelers' accounts of the* Hajj, *the grueling journey to Mecca, a centerpiece of the Muslim faith. Wolfe's own journey is recounted here.*

Yuse Medersa. He was fifty-five, a chunky man with baby-smooth skin and a hairline mustache. His store faced a busy square lined with vendors and fruit carts. I passed the place often. His floor stock never changed. In a storefront window misted with red dust were on display his few more modern items — three transistor radios, a videotape machine, two cassette recorders, and a color television. These never sold. . . . The shop did well because Abd-al-Hadi could fix whatever you brought him. I never saw him sell a retail item. The real money, you felt, was in repairs.

Indoors, behind a waist-high counter, stacks of used equipment rose to the roof beams, and forests of wiring dangled everywhere. Vintage amplifiers sat balanced on torn speakers at odd angles. Empty TV consoles, rainbows of circuitry poking out the backs, leaned against piled crates of picture tubes. Because the dirham abroad is all but worthless, Moroccans (who save the flints from disposable lighters) do not easily part with imported goods. No matter how outmoded, when a piece of equipment fails, they bring it into stores like Abd al-Hadi's. The entire shop was twenty-five feet square.

Although he went to Mecca often, Abd al-Hadi was only marginally well off. Unable to take much profit from his shop, he paid for the journeys by acting as a guide to first-time pilgrims. This year, for instance, he had three women, a trio of rich sisters, lined up as clients. He was still arranging their plane tickets when we met. The first week after Ramadan, I found him filling out visa applications, which he posted the next day to Rabat. The following week he proudly showed me a return-mail packet of beribboned papers. I naturally took an interest in all this, having as yet no visa of my own. . . .

I asked Abd al-Hadi about his Mecca clients.

"Very old," he said. "One is blind. None of them has even a living brother. They want to go to Mecca before they die, and I have been there. *Alors*, they bought me a ticket. As their escort."

Like most religious journeys, the Hajj has been bound up with trade since it began. I wondered if he would do a little business.

"*Bien sur*. The oil economy make equipment cheap there. I'll bring back a couple of cameras, a TV."

I tried to picture Abd al-Hadi leading his trio through the heat waves, shouldering a twenty-on- inch screen. He wrote on a card the name of his hotel in downtown Mecca. I said, *Insh' Allah*, I would look them up. . . .

Islamic law requires the Hajj of those who can afford it. Its rewards act as a goad to the middle classes. All over Morocco, men work hard, sometimes for years, acquiring the economic edge to leave their shops for a spell and go to Mecca. Prior to airplanes, when the journey was more daunting, requiring months and sometimes years of travel, the pilgrim returned with elevated status. Nowadays the rewards are more person-al. One's neighbors still pay attention when the suitcases come out, but a fiftyfold increase in hajjis has made the trip less impressive. These days one goes to fulfill a major obliga-tion, to round out one's life, to renew one's spirit, often damp-ened in the swamps of commerce. Some mourn the passing of older, slower ways. Many feel it is better. Moroccans are family-oriented people. The airplane reduces the trek to a three-week absence, and more pilgrims with less money can undertake it. They go to complete a set of rites and to see the place they have bowed toward for a lifetime. They come home with a title in front of their names: al-Hajj.

The Hajj is the fifth pillar of Islam. No one I encountered planned to miss it. Even sophisticated city dwellers viewed the rite as transformative: Your life could be changed by it forever. Elias Canetti had got it right in his book *Crowds and Power*: In the minds of most contemporary Muslims, you hadn't really lived till you'd made the Hajj.

Among Moroccans too poor to afford the trip, there were stories of miraculous transportations, astral projections, and magic-carpet rides to the holy shrine. These tales grow more plentiful the farther one lives from Mecca. Edward Westermarck's three-volume *Ritual and Belief in Morocco* retails dozens:

> One of [Sidi Hamed Buqudja's] followers expressed a wish to go to Mecca. The saint told him to go to the sea and throw himself in the water. He went there but could not persuade himself to follow the saint's advise. . . . A man came riding on horseback and asked him what he was doing. On hearing that . . . he would reach Mecca if he threw himself into the sea, the horseman fearlessly rode into the water. The saint, who was hidden in the sea, at once took the horse with the rider on his shoulders and carried them to Mecca.

In other stories, the shrine is brought to you:

> Moulay M'sish once told some of his followers to
> go with him to the top of the mountain . . . because he
> wanted to show them from there the Great Mosque in
> Mecca, and so he did. . . .
> Sidi al-Hajj al-Arbi of Wazzan caused the Ka'ba to
> come to Wazzan and walk around him seven times,
> just as the pilgrims walk around the Ka'ba in Mecca.

Originally instructive devices rather like Zen koans, stories like theses were first invented to internalize a spiritual message. Later they became a part of local folklore and were accepted at face value or as hagiography. . . .

Jidda Airport

I HAD CHOSEN MOROCCO as my starting point because it was familiar territory. Previous vistis over the years had accustomed me to its widely varied landscapes, its delicate foods, and its ancient mores. I was able to bargain in the local language and count in dirhams in my sleep. I know the alleys of the major cities. I had friends there.

In Saudi Arabia, I knew nobody. I had never even been inside the country. I was only going now to perform a demanding set of rites whose complexities already made me nervous. I did not intend to add to this the task of measuring deserts or assessing its people. I would not be traveling, in any case. I would be almost exclusively in Mecca,

Muhammad's birthplace and the least representative of
Saudi cities.

As the airplane took off, I steeled myself a little. . . . Scattered here and there across the aisles were the makings of a
group of men with whom I was going to spend the next
month in Mecca. But I did not know that yet. The sun rolled
down behind us, tinting the Red Sea a violent orange.
Nobody spoke.

We landed about 8:00 P.M. at the Hajj airport in Jidda,
and I followed a planeload of pilgrims down the ramps. The
women among us were scarved and wore white caftans.
Every man had on the white *ihram* garments. . . . The lower
wrap fell from my waist to my shins. The top half hung
loosely off the shoulders. This sacramental dress, ancient
and pastoral, is a common motif on Sumerian statuary dating to 2000 B.C.E. Against the airport's high-tech background, we looked like shepherds emerging from a steam
bath. The muggy Red Sea heat is legendary. I broke into a
sweat leaving the plane.

We entered a stadium-size concourse full of hajjis. I
stopped in my towels to gawk at the wing-spread roofs.
Tented on all sides, they gave the effect of a Bedouin
encampment. In overall area, this is the world's biggest airport. . . . This year, in a period of six weeks, a million pilgrims were going to set down here, a jumbo jet every five
minutes, four thousand hajjis every hour. It was also the
world's only "annual" airport, its systems too specialized to
handle normal traffic. At the end of the season, a few weeks
hence, the whole complex would close until next year.

Our group divided and subdivided, moving down the mall. I passed through customs, then joined a knot of three dozen pilgrims in a hallway. A Lebanese man with a curved stick took the lead. I had seen him on the airplane, wearing loafers and a Western business suit. (Now he sported the white *ihram*.) His staff was a saw on a pole, for pruning trees. His name was Mohamad Mardini. Offhand, cherubic, in his thirties, he seemed to know more than the others where we were going. The saw, he said, was a gift for a friend in the city. Its blade was covered by a cardboard scabbard. Walking I kept my eye on him in the crowds. If we fell behind, he raised the saw to direct us. . . .

Driving into the Hijaz

THE NIGHT WAS MOONLESS. Freeway lighting curtained off the land, Where it died away, I saw high desert dotted with scrub thorn bushes and steppe grass. The road curved up through switchbacks flattened to a plain, the climbed again. Isolated peaks poked up like islands. Now and then in fields beside the road, we passed small herds of camel. Oddly formal looking in the headlights, they raised their heads from grazing as we passed.

As we rode along, the men began chanting the Talbiyya:

I am here to serve you, Allah. Here I am!
I am here because nothing compares to you.
Here I am!
Praise blessings, and the kingdom are yours.
Nothing compares to you.

These lines are the Hajj's hallmark, as much as the *ihram*. I heard them repeated day and night for weeks. The fifth line, echoing the second, wrapped back on the first line like an English round. The Arabic is chanted . . . *Talbiyya* means "to wait, in a ready state, for an order or direction." One of its functions is to clear the mind, to prepare you for anything. In the van, it began the moment we left the airport. Before long, I would hear it in my dreams.

The *ihram* had a powerful impact on me, too. For one thing, it put an end to my months of arrangements. In a way, it put an end to me as well. The uniform cloth defeats class distinctions and cultural fashion. Rich and poor are lumped together in it, looking like penitents in a Bosch painting. The *ihram* is as democratic as a death shroud. This, I learned later, is intentional.

Mecca lies fifty miles east of the Red Sea. It is a modern city of one million people, splashing up the rim of a granite bowl a thousand feet above sea level. Barren peaks surround it on every side, but there are passes: one leading north toward Syria; one south to Yemen: one west to the coast. A fourth, a ring road, runs east to Ta'if. By day, the hills form a volcanic monotony. At night they blend into the sky and disappear.

The first thing I discovered about Mecca was that I'd been spelling the name wrong. West of town we passed a fluorescent sign with glowing arrows and six letters sparkling in the headlights: MAKKAH. The orthography threw me. With it two hard *c*'s, Mecca is the most loaded Arabic word in the English language. Without them, what is it? No one here said

MEH-ka. They said ma-KAH. The accent took getting used to, but English-speaking Meccans insisted on it. "Do you pronounce Manhattan men-HET-en?" one of them asked me.

A title was linked to Mecca on every road sign: al-Mukarraman, the Ennobled. With its special laws of sanctuary, with its status as the birthplace of Islam, the city is sacred ground, however you spell it. It is also strictly off-limits to nonbelievers. Another sign, at a freeway exit read:

STOP FOR INSPECTION

ENTRY PROHIBITED TO NON-MUSLIMS

The van rolled to a stop beneath the sign. Two soldiers stepped out of a booth and played their flashlights through the cab. Visas were checked. The Hajjis continued chanting. A few looked nervous.

Some Westerners think of Mecca as forbidden to foreigners. In fact, it exists to receive them and is largely composed of them. Most of the populace descends through thirteen centuries of migrant pilgrims who settled here after their Hajj and did not go home. The result is a cosmopolitan city, where every nation and race has taken root. Naturally it is completely Muslim. Only a Muslim has any business being there.

The officers brought back our passports in a basket. We left the checkpoint and continued on. Hijazi landscapes are studies in barren grimness. It was hard to imagine a sanctuary among the mangled limbs of Mother Nature. Bare hills rose in the headlights — treeless ridges reminiscent of Death Valley. The skyline looked straight out of Stephen Crane:

On the horizon
The peaks assembled;
And as I looked,
The march of the mountains began.
Ant as they marched, they sang,
"Ay! ,we come! we come!"

At the top of a final ridge, the road swept east and joined a freeway. The asphalt here was lit up like an airfield. Luminescence bathed the rubbled hills; then, at blinding speed, the van shot under a giant concrete book. I swung around in disbelief, staring back through the windows. There it stood: a sculpture the size of an overpass, a Claes Oldenburg mirage of huge arched crossbeams supporting a forty-ton Quran. Did you see that? Then we came over the lip of a canyon. The lights of Mecca lay fanned out in a bowl. . . .

Arriving in Mecca

THAT SAME NIGHT, we were climbing with the crowds up Umm al-Qura Road. At the top of the rise, where the street was closed to cars, a throng of five thousand people moved up the pavement. Reaching the crest, I came up on my toes. Everyone knew what was down there, glowing at the bottom of the valley: the largest open-air temple in the world.

I fell in behind Mardini as we climbed. Soon I was being introduced to a Saudi guide named Shaykh Ibrahim, a professor of *hadith* at the local university. I asked him what the

Prophet has said about the mosque. . . .

Ibrahim was a gentle man, the most taciturn of the four guides attached to our party. A few blocks farther on I asked again.

He said, "Just remember: the Ka'ba is a sacred building. But not so sacred as the people who surround it," and pointing to the ground, he made a circle with his finger. "Whatever you do here, don't hurt anyone, not even accidentally. We are going to perform the Umra now. We will greet the mosque, circle the Shrine, walk seven times between the hills, like Hagar. Think of it as a pilgrim's dress rehearsal. Don't rush, don't push. Take it easy. Get out of the way if anyone acts wild. If you harm someone, your performance might not be acceptable. You might do it for nothing."

Shaykh Ibrahim's explanation of the Umra . . . was the longest single speech I would hear him make in the next four weeks. The view from the brow of the hill cut off further discussion. Behind a concrete overpass rose the biggest minaret I'd ever seen.

Down below, a mosque in the shape of a mammoth door key completely filled the hollow. Lit from above, roofless at the center, it seemed to enclose the valley bowl it covered. The proportions of this eccentric structure were staggering. The head of the key alone comprised a corral of several acres. In addition, attached to the east wall, the shaft of a two-story concourse ran on another quarter mile. For so much stone, the effect at night, beneath banks of floods, was airy, glowing, tentlike. Seven minarets pegged down the sides.

This was the recent surrounding mosque that encapsulates

a much older Ottoman courtyard. Ibrahim called it Haram al-Sharif, the Noble Sanctuary. Its 160,000 [square] yards of floor provided room on a crowded day, for 1.2 million pilgrims. Galleries lit up the second story. Parapets ran right around the roof. From the crest of the hill, the minarets looked canted. I could not begin to guess the building's height. Its outer walls were faced in polished slabs of blue-gray marble, and the marine shades differed stone to stone. The veins shooting through them looked like ruffled surf. The minarets were spotlighted. On every side, the valley glowed.

I had never seen such a beguiling temple complex. Saint Peter's Basilica in Rome is roofed, and open to tourists. Palenque [in Mexico] covers more ground, but no one uses it. My aversion to sightseeing vanished before this pool of light and stone. All the must-see points were in one building.

We followed the road downhill beneath a bridge. Chunks of the mosque heaved into view as we went down, here a gallery, there a tower, shifting behind facades and concrete rooftops. The the street curved sharply, and the building disappeared.

A hot breeze swept down the hillside. Behind, the hum of traffic died away. The lots, where cars and buses parked at quieter times of the year, were occupied tonight by camping pilgrims. Fires burned low between the groups. Bedrolls lay open under bridgeheads. At the edge of the road, we came upon a circle of Ghanaians reciting the Qur'an around a lamp. Most of the encampment was asleep now.

We entered a canyon lined with bazaars and food stalls. Where it leveled out, the mosque returned to view. Its second floor had a Coliseum-like curve to the upper galleries. Across the road we stopped before a gate, forming a huddle. Ibrahim addressed us. . . .When everything was settled, we waded into the crowds around the mosque.

The Mosque

MOST HAJJIS ARRIVING at Mecca enter the Haram through Bab al-Salaam, the Gate of Peace. Ibn Battuta went in by this gate; so did Ibn Jubayr, his predecessor. . . . Tonight crowds on the stairs kept us from fulfilling this tradition.

Mardini shrugged. We continued around the mosque to another gate, Bab al-Malik. A shallow flight of steps led up to a foyer. We deposited our sandals at the door and stepped across the threshold, right foot first.

Inside we offered the formulaic greeting:

This is your sanctuary.
This is your city.
I am your servant.
Peace is your.
You are salvation.
Grant us salvation,
And guide us
Through the gates of Paradise.

Crossing the foyer, we entered a series of pillared, curving halls. In surrounding naves lit by chandeliers, fields of

pilgrim families sat on carpets, reclining, conversing, reading the Qur'an. Their numbers increased as we moved deeper
into the building. Books on waist-high shelves divided quiet
colonnades. Brass fixtures overhead were interspersed with
fans lazily turning. We continued down an aisle through the
crowds. The Ka'ba, Islam's devotional epicenter, stood in an
open courtyard dead ahead, but we could not see it. There
were three hundred thousand pilgrims in the complex. Our
walk from the outer gate took fifteen minutes.

The colonnades enclose an oval floor of about four acres.
The oldest columns in the mosque flank the perimeter,
columns that Burckhardt, Burton, al-Fasi, and Qutb al-Din
all felt compelled to count and could never agree on. On the
east wing, they stood in quadruple rows; elsewhere they ran
three deep into the building, making a courtyard portico.

I had read about this building and glimpsed it on Moroccan television, but taking its measure now was out of the
question. Its proportions could not compete with its population, or with the emotional state of those I saw. To begin
with, the aisles and carpets held an astounding racial micro-
cosm: Berbers, Indians, Sudanese, Yemenis, Malaysians,
and Pakistanis overlapped Nigerians, Indonesians, Baluchis,
Bangladeshis, Turks, Iraqis, and Kurds. It was a calm crowd
with almost no pushing. Our numbers did not result in agita-
tion. The rush to reach Mecca was finished. The hajjis had
arrived. Now the laws of sanctuary took over. This was the
peace we had petitioned in the foyer. Everyone felt it.

Across the way a vigorous-looking Afghan in his eighties,
six feet tall with burnished skin, stood praying into his open

hands while big tears dropped onto his palms. A deep exhilaration knocked at my rib cage. Counting up columns in this became absurd.

The Tawaf

AS WE WALKED, the aisles were subtly descending, conforming to the valley floor. We passed out of the covered portico and stepped down into the marble courtyard. This was the head of the key, the building's hub.

[All the other mosques in the world are] arranged in figures of four sides. The core of the mosque at Mecca is on the round, an open, roofless forum overlooked by tiered arcades. The marble floor is 560 feet on the long sides, 350 feet wide, and polished to the whiteness of an ice rink. At the center of this hub stands the Ka'ba, a four-story cube of rough granite covered in a black embroidered veil.

This monolith is Islam's most sacred shrine. Thomas Carlyle, the Scottish historian, called it an authentic fragment of the oldest past. It was already ancient when Muhammad's grandfather restored it in 580 C.E. Its tall simplicity and black refection lend the mass an upward rhythm. Tonight a light breeze ruffled its cover, and the slabs felt strangely cool beneath my feet. After acres of ceilings, it was soothing to look up and see some stars.

We were fifty or sixty yards from the Ka'ba, moving around the outskirts of the forum. Knots of hajjis, stopped in their tracks, stood everywhere around. The first sight of the Shrine was literally stunning. Men wept and muttered verses where they stood. Women leaned against columns, crying the rarest sort of tears — of safe arrival, answered prayers, gratified desire. I shared these emotions. I also felt an urge to escape my skin, to swoop through the crowd like lines in a Whitman poem, looking out of every pilgrim's eyeballs. I heard [a fellow pilgrim named] Fayez call out as he hurried past, "We made it! We made it!"

A doughnut ring of pilgrims ten rows deep circled the Shrine, forming a revolving band of several thousand people. We kept to the edge of them, skirting the cube, and faced its eastern corner. Here a black stone in a silver bezel had been set into an angle of the building. This was its oldest relic, the lodestone of popular Islam. We faced the stone and stated our intention:

Allah, I plan to circle your Sacred House.
Make it easy for me,
And accept
My seven circuits in your name.

Each hajji began at the Black Stone and circled the Ka'ba counterclockwise. . . . At a distance, the wheeling pilgrims obscured its base, so that for a moment the block itself appeared to be revolving on its axis. As we came nearer, the Shrine increased dramatically in size. On the edge of the ring, we adjusted our *ihrams* and raised our hands to salute the Stone. Then we joined the circle.

Keeping the Shrine on our left, we began to turn. Ibrahim and Mardini went ahead, calling words over their shoulders as we followed. There were special supplications for every angle of the building, but not many pilgrims had them memorized. Now and then we passed someone reading set prayers from a handbook, but most people were speaking from the heart. I caught up to Mardini and asked him what was proper. The invocations all but drowned us out. "One God, many tongues!" he shouted. "Say what you want, or repeat what you hear. Or just say, 'God is great.'" I dropped back into the wheel and did all three.

The first three circuits of *tawaf* are performed at a brisk pace called *ramal*, or "moving the shoulders as if walking in sand." Richard Burton likened the step to the *pas gymnastique*. I had not imagined the Hajj would be so athletic. Each time a circuit returned to the Stone, it was all I could do to remember to raise my palms and shout, *"Allahu akbar!"* It was not the pace or the distance but the crowd that was distracting. On the perimeter of the ring, I noticed wooden litters passing, on which pilgrims weakened by age or illness were being borne around. These pallets marked the circle's outer edges.

Coming around the northwest wall, we included in each circuit a half circle of floor marked by a rail. Inside the rail lay two slabs of green stone said to mark the graves of Hagar and Ishmael. Directly above, a delicate golden rainspout protruded from the roof of the Ka'ba. The prayer at this spot alluded to the rainspout:

On that day
When the only shade is yours,
Take me into your shadow, Lord,

and let me drink
From the Prophet's trough
To quench my thirst forever.

The liturgy and the place were of a piece here.

We performed the quicker circuits near the Ka'ba, on the inside rim of the doughnut. When they were done, Mardini began taking side steps, distancing himself from the Shrine as we moved along. I followed suit, working my way to the outer edge of the circle, where we performed our last four rounds at a leisurely walk.

As the pace fell off, space opened around us. I could see the black drape rustle on a breeze. It hung down the Ka'ba on all sides, covering the cube in heavy silk. Its name is *al-kiswa*. I later heard it called the Shrine's *ihram*.

The Zamzam Well

ONE HAD TO PERFORM the *tawaf* to comprehend it. Its choreographic message, with God's House at the center, only came clear to me in the final rounds. Orbiting shoulder to shoulder with so many others induced in the end an open heart and a mobile point of view.

The final circuit brought us back to the eastern corner. We saluted the Black Stone as we swept past, then washed up on an outer bank of marble, behind a copper enclosure the size of a phone booth. This was called the Station of Abraham. Prayers offered here acquired special grace. We faced the Ka'ba and performed two *rakats* together.

Our rite of *tawaf* was complete now, but the evening was not over. Next we descended a flight of steps to a cavernous room containing the Zamzam Well. Cool air flooded the stairwell, cutting the night's heat as we went down.

In Ibn Battuta's day, the Zamzam Well was housed above ground in a large pavilion. Today, the floor has been cleared of these installations. The water drawers and leather buckets have vanished, too, and the profiteers who placed exorbitant fees on the concession. Even the well has been relocated, to a wedge-shaped amphitheater underground.

The air was deliciously damp the first night I went down there. The slanting stone floors ran with surplus water. Hajjis not content merely to drink dumped buckets of the liquid on their bodies, and strangers toweled off each other's backs. The atmosphere was like a friendly bathhouse. Here and there, on a dry patch, lay a solitary sleeper. . . .

Mecca would not exist without this well. Its appearance in the bone-dry Hajiz is a fundamental wonder: the first condition of desert urban life. For thousands of years, it supplied the whole town for drinking and ablutions. Seeing it, I understood why Muhammad had linked water to prayer and installed a purifying rite at the heart of his practice. Even in pre-Islamic times, the well was sacramental. Today, pilgrims drink from it to fulfill tradition. Minerals render it heavy, but I found the taste of Zamzam water sweet, not brackish, and very,very cold (its having passed through a cooling system in the basement). . . .

The Sa'y

OUR LAST LABOR of the night was a ritual jog between the hills. The rite, called *sa'y*, takes place in the concourse on the long side of the key. To reach it, we crossed the Ka'ba floor, saluted the Stone, then walked out of the courtyard, heading south.

A series of arches led through cloisters to a gate. Here the head of the mosque and its shaft were joined, forming a marble lane called the Masa'a. Later I heard one hajji refer to it as the racecourse. I was unprepared for the length of this passage: a quarter-mile stretch of covered mall, split in two lanes for pilgrims coming and going.

The course began at the top of a hill called Safa, jutting from the base of Mount Qubays. It ended at the second hill, Marwa, in the north of the building. I had never seen hillocks housed inside a building; domes had been set in the ceilings to accommodate their crowns. A complete lap covered about eight hundred yards. Here, as around the Ka'ba, old age and illness were shown consideration. Down the center of the Masa'a, on a median strip dividing the two lanes, frail pilgrims were being wheeled in rented chairs.

Saluting the Shrine at the top of each relay, we completed seven lengths, or about two miles. My legs began to throb in the third round. The contrast between the mystical *tawaf* and this linear, headlong rush could not have been greater. Wandering loosely between fixed points, doubling back on itself around the hills, the rite expressed persistence and survival. The *sa'y* was not a circle dance. Its intent seemed to be to instill compassion for the victimized and exiled. This was the mall of necessitous desire.

We finished our run and stepped down onto a ramp beside al-Marwa. By now, our *ihram* towels were streaked with dirt and sweat. We had come through the Umra. We were *muta'ammirin*. As we stood shaking hands (Mohamed Fayez high-fived me), two self-appointed barbers stepped from the wings, offering their services. In order to put aside the *ihram* clothes, a pilgrim who plans to return to them for the Hajj is supposed to have a desacralizing haircut. Generally this means a token snip of three or four neck hairs. When it was done, we returned to Bab al-Malik for our sandals. . . .

Mecca to Minna Valley

THE SKY WAS GROWING red as we climbed on the bus. We had been coming to this moment for a week now. We were leaving for the desert. As the bus swayed forward through thick traffic, the mosque fell behind. At times, the pedestrian crowds moved faster than we did. With stops, we averaged fifteen miles an hour.

It was hard to imagine a time when the Hajj had not been up on wheels. Four-lane bands of glinting chrome snaked up the hillsides. Crowds dashed between bumpers. Vehicles spilled off the modern roads, taking shortcuts over sand and scabblings. In a little more than fifty years, a medieval city had been utterly transformed by modern transportation. I wondered what would come when the car was gone. It would take a lot more than a face-lift to rearrange things.

The town had been remade for the rubber tire, the wider axle. A massive infrastructure of tunnels, freeways, and overpasses swooping impressively through granite hills physically walled us off from the 1930s, when the Hajj was still an occasion of the camel. Harry St. John Philby wrote then of the Mina caravan, "There must have been fifty thousand of them at least, and all moving forward together at the silent, hurried pace characteristic of the chief carrier of Arabia."

Today's chief carrier ran on gasoline. Bumper to bumper the trade-off appeared pathetic, and yet we were not figures in a frieze. The Hajj had been motorized for fifty years, and we were products of that history, a part of the blaring horns and squealing rubber, not the sweep of padded feet.

A camel can carry four hundred pounds of cargo, cover sixty miles a day for twenty days without a drink in temperatures of 120 degrees Fahrenheit — and still go five more days before it dies. Only a fool is not respectful of the camel. On the other hand, almost no one on the bus knew how to ride one. Rafiq, [a] Libyan, who did, only joked about it: "Imagine yourselves on that wooden saddle, wearing cotton towels! . . . "

Makkah

AS MY STAY WOUND down in Mecca, I spent more time [at the Haram], marking my notebooks, meditating, reading. I strolled, performed my circuits, sat and watched. At mealtimes, I ducked out of the mosque to eat from wooden stalls in the jewelry market.

I [now possessed] an overview of the Hajj different from the Hajj I had imagined, and I wanted to fix it while my thoughts were fresh. I began to fill a notebook with summations. From California, I had viewed the Hajj as a journey to a physical destination. In fact, the Hajj was protean, all process. It surprised me now to see how off I'd been. In the West, the notion of pilgrimage centered on going, on reaching, on arrival. Nailing this moribund image to the Hajj was a mistake, like claiming that going home to dinner began with getting off work and ended when you reached the porch — omitting any mention of the meal.

Reaching Mecca was only a beginning. The goal of the Hajj was to perform it well. The rites were hard, sometimes unfathomable — like living. Yet they provided a counterweight to the usual view of life as a dog-and-cat fight. Elsewhere, except at the best of times, every person looked out for himself. During the Hajj, people looked out for each other. The Hajj is a shared rite of passage. I saw it through the eyes of others as much as through my own. In that way, it was like an act of love. . . .

I especially admired the way the sweat and the symbols flowed together. By an act of imagination and exertion, a spiritual rite of some duration fulfilled a private quest. For all its public aspects, the experience was intensely personal. By giving the pilgrim a chance to choose his moment, it provided a service missing in the West since the days of the medieval palmers: It offered a climax to religious life.

THE
PEOPLE

MARK SINGER

Islam in America

HE MIGRATION OF Arabs to Detroit
in measurable numbers began in the early
twentieth century. The first wave of immigrants were mostly Christians from Syria
and what is now Lebanon. Muslims,
attracted by job opportunities in the automobile industry,
started appearing not long thereafter, and since the sixties they
have predominated, arriving in ripples that emanate from cat-
aclysms in the Middle East — an
influx of Palestinians after 1967,
followed by Lebanese refugees
during the late seventies and early
eighties, and Iraqi Shiites in the
early nineties. Nothing about the
local scenery reminded the earliest arrivals of home, but today certain run-down pockets of southeast Dearborn look as if they

MARK SINGER *has
been a staff writer for*
The New Yorker *for
the last twenty-five years.
Since September 11,
he has profiled Arabs
in the United States,
including this piece on
Dearborn, Michigan,
the largest
Arab-American
community in the
United States.*

might have been grafted on from the West Bank, and in the middle-class neighborhoods there are long commercial stretches with store signs in both Arabic and English. An average of five thousand new Arab immigrants make Detroit their port of entry each year.

In Dearborn, as in New York City, September 11 was a mayoral primary-election day. Unlike New York, Dearborn kept its polls open. The incumbent, Michael Guido, was seeking a fifth term, and although he received 60 percent of the vote, the rules mandate a November runoff against the second-place finisher, Abed Hammoud, a thirty-five-year-old assistant prosecutor, who got 18 percent. Hammoud, who is Lebanese, immigrated to the United States in 1990, and likes to say that he landed in America "three days after Saddam moved into Kuwait." This dash of rhetorical color won't hurt with the Iraqi refugee vote, but he would pick that up anyway. Not that it will be enough. No one, with the possible exception of Hammoud himself, expects him to win.

For a small-city mayor, Guido, a stocky fellow in his mid-forties who favors pin-striped suits, suspenders, and monogrammed shirts with French cuffs, has been quite adept at cultivating an old-school big-city mayoral persona. During his first campaign, in 1985, he circulated a blunt-talking pamphlet that referred to Dearborn's "Arab Problem," in which he disparaged bilingual classes for Arab children in the public schools, "new neighbors [who] neglect their property," and the "'gimme, gimme, gimme" attitude" of "the so-called leadership" of the Arab community. Some Dearborn

Arabs with long memories place Guido on a continuum that extends back to the heyday of Orville Hubbard, an unapologetic segregationist who was mayor from 1942 to 1977. (Hubbard is most often remembered for promoting the unsubtle motto "Keep Dearborn Clean"and for his role during the 1967 race riots in Detroit, when he took to the street to prohibit blacks from crossing into his city.) Guido has sufficient finesse to have befriended many members of the older Lebanese business establishment. But no one would accuse him of being overly solicitous toward the larger Arab population, and they are grossly underrepresented in the municipal workforce — about 2.5 percent.

Dearborn is arguably the most likely city in America where a mayoral candidate, after outlining his position on street-light maintenance, might be tossed questions about national security and would be expected to answer. Guido knows that most voters aren't all that concerned with local politics at the moment and that the less he says the better. The terrorist attack, he said, "clouds what you can do to separate yourself from your opponent." He continued, "You don't point out that your opponent is Arab-American. You talk about what you can do. What I've done for my city, I blow this guy out of the water — that should be the contest. But, you know, I have people saying, 'I'm voting for you because I don't want to vote for an Arab.' Three people have told me that in the last week. Three people telling you that out loud is like getting ten letters. And the politician's rule of thumb is that ten letters means a thousand people are thinking about it."

Or, as Hammoud said to me the week after the attack, "You think I can go knock on doors now? It's not a good time to campaign."

In the spring of 1991, after participating in uprisings against the government of Saddam Hussein, Abu Muslim al-Hayder, a Shiite college professor of computer-control engineering who was then in his mid-thirties, fled Iraq with his wife and four children. They had not been long inside a Saudi Arabian refugee camp when it became evident that it was hardly a refuge. The camp population was infested with spies for the Saddam regime and "the Saudis don't look at us as full human beings — they look at us as prisoners."After the family spent a year and a half in detention, a relief agency called the Church World Service resettled them in Washington State. There al-Hayder went back to school and subsequently tried and failed to find a job in the computer industry. Confident that his bilingual abilities made him employable, in 1995 he moved the family to Detroit.

On September 11, al-Hayder, who has been a citizen for five years, happened to be one of the federal observers dispatched to monitor the municipal election in the town of Hamtramck, ten miles northeast of Dearborn, where there had been discrimination against Arab voters in the past. He was supposed to spend that night in a hotel and file a report the next morning, but he was allowed to leave at 9 P.M. and return to his wife and (now six) children, in Detroit.

"I found all my family scared, afraid that somebody would attack the house,"he told me. Most of his neighbors had American flags displayed on their porches, and when he went to a flag store the next day it was sold out. As a short-term approach to making his allegiance plain, he tied an American-flag balloon to his balcony.

Before September 11, al-Hayder said, he felt happy and secure. He was delighted with his children's progress in school and, in his work as ACCESS's professional liaison to the Iraqi community, he was gratified by the chance to help his newly arrived countrymen. He counts himself far more fortunate than many other erstwhile Iraqi professionals—the college teacher who now delivers pizzas; the widely published literary critic who, having failed at carpentry, is now on welfare. But he is also greatly disturbed by the American media's depiction of Muslims, most of all because of how it might affect his children's perception of themselves.

Al-Hayder has a long familiarity with, and an exceptional equanimity in the face of, the consequences of dissent. In 1978, he was imprisoned by Saddam's predecessor, Ahmad Hassan al-Bakr, and sentenced to death for his political associations, then released a year and a half later when Saddam came to power and issued an amnesty for most political prisoners. Al-Hayder remembers regarding the gesture with skepticism. "I didn't trust Saddam," he said, "because I knew that even if he gives you something he will take a lot of things more valuable."

If he saved your life, I asked, how could he take from you something more valuable?

"There are many things more valuable than your life. There is your dignity, your respect. If you live a life with no respect, it's better to die. And this is why I agreed to come to

America as a refugee — better than to stay in Saudi Arabia or go to another country. But this crisis we are in is making many people, especially the media, turn away from the values that I know. If someone comes and tries to insult me for no reason, I cannot tell him thank you. A lot of people now who are colored and are American citizens, and who have a right to have weapons, may go and get a license to have weapons to defend themselves. I may even lose faith in law-enforcement agencies because they target people who are Arab and Muslims. And this is very disturbing. None of this is why I came here. I came here to be a respected human being."

Islam in Iran

ASHIITE IS, first of all, a rabid opposi-
tionist. At first the Shiites were a small
group of the friends and backers of Ali,
the son-in-law of Muhammad and husband of the Prophet's beloved daughter
Fatima. When Muhammad died without a male heir and
without clearly designating his successor, the Muslims
began struggling over the Prophet's inheritance, over who
would be caliph, or leader of the
believers in Allah and thus the
most important person in the
Islamic world. Ali's party (*Shi'a*
means "party") supports its
leader for this position, maintain-
ing that Ali is the sole representative of the Prophet's family,
the father of Muhammad's two
grandsons, Hassan and Hussein.

RYSZARD KAPUŚCIŃSKI's
*account of Islam in Iran
is taken from his book*
Shah of Shahs, *a profile
of the Shah of Iran's last
days. Kapuściński,
an acclaimed Polish
journalist, has gained
critical and popular
praise for his coverage
of civil wars, revolutions,
and social conditions in
the Third World.*

The Sunni Muslim majority, however, ignores the voices of the Shiites for twenty-four years and chooses Abu Bakr, Umar, and Utman as the next three caliphs. Ali finally becomes caliph, but his caliphate ends after five years, when an assassin splits his skull with a poisoned saber. Of Ali's two sons, Hassan will be poisoned and Hussein will fall in battle. The death of Ali's family deprives the Shiites of the chance to win power, which passes to Sunni Omayyad, Abassid, and Ottoman dynasties. The caliphate, which Muhammad had conceived as a simple and modest institution, becomes a hereditary monarchy. In this situation the plebeian, pious, poverty-stricken Shiites, appalled by the nouveau-riche style of the victorious caliphs, go over to the opposition.

All this happens in the middle of the seventh century, but it has remained a living and passionately dwelt-on history to this day. When a devout Shiite talks about his faith he will constantly return to those remote histories and relate tearfully the massacre at Karbala in which Hussein had his head cut off. A skeptical, ironic European will think, God, what can any of that mean today? But if he expresses such thoughts aloud, he provokes the anger and hatred of the Shiite.

The Shiites have indeed had a tragic fate, and the sense of tragedy, of the historical wrongs and misfortunes that accompany them, is encoded deep within their consciousness. The world contains communities for whom nothing has gone right for centuries — everything has slipped through their hands, and every ray of hope has faded as soon as it began to shine — these people seem to bear some sort of fatal brand. So it is with the Shiites. For this reason, perhaps, they have an air of dead seriousness, of fervent unsettling adherence to their arguments and principles, and also (this is only an impression, of course) of sadness.

As soon as the Shiites (who constitute barely a tenth of all Muslims, the rest being Sunnis) go into opposition, the persecution begins. To this day they live the memory of the centuries of pogroms against them, and so they close themselves off in ghettos, use signals only they understand, and devise conspiratorial forms of behavior. But the blows keep falling on their heads.

Gradually they start to look for safer places where they will have a better chance of survival. In those times of difficult and slow communication, in which distance and space constitute an efficient isolator, a separating wall, the Shiites try to move as far as possible from the center of power (which lies first in Damascus and later in Baghdad). They scatter throughout the world, across mountains and deserts, and descend step by step underground. So the Shiite diaspora, which has lasted till today, comes into being. The epic of the Shiites is full acts of incredible abjuration, courage, and spiritual strength. A part of the wandering community heads east. Crossing the Tigris and the Euphrates, it passes through the mountains of Zagros and reaches the Iranian desert plateau.

At this time, Iran, exhausted and laid waste by centuries of war with Byzantium, has been conquered by Arabs who are spreading the new faith, Islam. This process is going on slowly, amid continual fighting. Until now the Iranians have had an official religion, Zoroastrianism, related to the ruling

Sassanid dynasty. Now comes the attempt to impose upon them another official religion, associated with a new and, what's more, a foreign regime — Sunni Islam. It seem like jumping from the frying pan into the fire.

But exactly at this moment the poor, exhausted, wretched Shiites, still bearing the visible traces of the Gehenna they have lived through, appear. The Iranians discover that these Shiites are Muslims and, additionally (as they claim), the only legitimate Muslims, the only preservers of a pure faith for which they are ready to give their lives. Well fine, say the Iranians — but what about your Arab brothers, who have conquered us? Brothers? cry the outraged Shiites. Those Arabs are Sunnis, usurpers and our persecutors. They murdered Ali and seized power. No, we don't acknowledge them. We are in opposition! Having made this proclamation, the Shiites ask if they might rest after their long journey and request a jug of cold water.

The pronouncement by the barefoot newcomers sets the Iranians thinking along important lines. You can be a Muslim without being an establishment Muslim. What's more, you can be an opposition Muslim! And that makes you an even better Muslim! They feel empathy for these poor, wronged Shiites. At this moment the Iranians themselves are poor and feel wronged. They have been ruined by war, and an invader controls their country. So they quickly find a common language with these exiles who are looking for shelter and counting on their hospitality. The Iranians begin to listen to the Shiite preachers and finally accept their faith.

In this adroit maneuver one can see all the intelligence and independence of the Iranians. They have a particular talent for preserving their independence under conditions of subjugation. For hundreds of years the Iranian have been the victims of conquest, aggression, and partition. They have been ruled for centuries on end by foreigners or local regimes dependent on foreign powers, and yet they have preserved their culture and language, their impressive personality, and so much spiritual fortitude that in propitious circumstances they can arise reborn from the ashes. During the twenty-five centuries of their recorded history the Iranians have always, sooner or later, managed to outwit anyone with the impudence to try ruling them. Sometimes they have to resort to the weapons of uprising and revolution to obtain their goal, and then they pay the tragic levy of blood. Sometimes they use the tactic of passive resistance, which they apply in a particularly consistent and radical way. When they get fed up with an authority that has become unbearable, the whole country freezes, the whole nation does a disappearing act. Authority gives orders but no one is listening, it frowns but no one is looking, it raises its voice but that voice is as one crying in the wilderness. Then authority falls apart like a house of cards. The most common Iranian technique, however, is absorption, active assimilation, in a way that turns the foreign sword into the Iranians' own weapon.

And so it is after the Arab conquest. You want Islam, they tell the conquers, so Islam you'll get — but in our own national form and in an independent, rebellious version. It will be faith, but an Iranian faith that expresses our spirit, our culture, and our independence. This philosophy underlies the

Iranian decision to accept Islam. They accept it in the Shiite variant, which at that time is the faith of the wronged and the conquered, an instrument of contestation and resistance, the ideology of the unhumbled who are ready to suffer but will not renounce their principles because they want to preserve their distinctness and dignity. Shiism will become not only the national religion of the Iranians but also their refuge and shelter, a form of national survival and, at the right moments, of struggle and liberation.

Iran transforms itself into the most restless province of the Muslim empire. Someone is always plotting here, there is always some uprising, masked messengers appear and disappear, secret leaflets and brochures circulate. The representatives of the occupying authorities, the Arab governors, spread terror and end up with results opposite to what they'd intended. In answer to the official terror the Iranian Shiites begin to fight back, but not in a frontal assault, for which they are too weak. An element of the Shiite community from now on will be — if one can use such a term — the terrorist fringe. Down to the present day, small conspiratorial terrorist organizations that know neither fear nor pity operate in Iran. Half of the killings blamed on the ayatollahs are performed on the sentences of these groups. Generally, history regards the Shiites as the founders of the theory and practice of individual terror as a means of combat.

Fervor, orthodoxy, and an obsessive, fanatic concern for doctrinal purity characterize the Shiites as they characterize every group that is persecuted, condemned to the ghetto, and made to fight for its survival. A persecuted man cannot survive without an unshakable faith in the correctness of his choice. He must protect the values that led him to that choice. Thus, all the schisms — and Shiism has lived through dozen of them — had one thing in common: They were all, as we would put it, ultra-leftist. A fanatical branch was always springing up to accuse the remainder of its co-religionists of atrophied zeal, of treating lightly the dictates of faith, of expediency and taking the easy way out. Once the split took place the fervid of the schismatics would take up arms to finish off the enemies of Islam, redeeming in blood (because they themselves often perished) the treachery and laziness of their backsliding brothers.

The Iranian Shiites have been living underground, in the catacombs, for eight hundred years. Their life recalls the suffering and trials of the first Christians. Sometimes it seems that they will be extirpated completely, that a final annihilation awaits them. For years they have been taking refuge in the mountains, holing up in caves, dying of hunger. Their songs that survive from these years, full of rue and despair, prophesy the end of the world.

But there have also been calmer periods, and then Iran became the refuge of all the oppositionists in the Muslim empire, who arrive from all corners of the world to find shelter, encouragement, and support among the plotting Shiites. They could also take lessons in the great Shiite school of conspiracy. They might, for example, master the principle of disassembling (*taqija*), which facilitates survival. This principle allow the Shiite, when he finds himself up against a stronger opponent, seemingly to accept the prevailing religion and acclaim himself a believer as long as doing so will save him and his people. Shiism also teaches *kitman*, the art of disorienting one's enemies, which allows the Shiite to contradict his own assurances and pretend that he is an idiot when danger threatens. Iran thus becomes a medieval mecca of malcontents, rebels, strange varieties of hermits, prophets, ecstatics, shady heretics, stigmatics, mystics, and fortunetellers, who pour in along every road to teach, contemplate, pray, and soothsay. All this creates the atmosphere of religiosity, exaltation, and mysticism so characteristic of the country. I was very devout in school, say an Iranian, and all the kids thought I had a radiant halo around my head. Try imagining a European leader who writes that once when he was out riding he fell over a cliff and would have died except that a saint reached out a hand to save him. Yet the last Shah described such a scene in a book of his and all Iran read it seriously. Superstitious beliefs, such as faith in numbers, omens, symbols, prophecies, and revelations have deep roots here.

In the sixteenth century the rulers of the Safavid dynasty raised Shiism to the dignity of official religion. What had been the ideology of mass opposition became the ideology of a state in opposition — for the Iranian state opposed the Sunni domination of the Ottoman Empire. But with time the relations between the monarchy and Shiism grew worse and worse.

The point is that Shiites not only reject the authority of the caliphs; they barely tolerate any lay authority at all. Iran constitutes the unique case of a country whose people believe only in the reign of their religious leaders, the imams, one of whom, the last, left this world (according to rational, if not to Shiite, criteria) in the ninth century.

Here we reach the essence of Shiite doctrine, the main act of faith for its believers. Deprived of any chance to win the caliphate, the Shiites turn their backs on the caliphs and henceforth acknowledge only the leaders of their own faith, the imams. Ali is the first imam. Hassan and Hussein his sons the second and third, and so on until the twelfth. All these imams died violent deaths at the hands of caliphs who saw them as dangerous rivals. The Shiites believe, however, that the twelfth and last imam, Muhammad, did not perish but disappeared into the cave under the great mosque at Samarra, in Iraq. This happened in 878. He is the Hidden Imam, the Awaited One, who will appear at the appropriate time as Mahdi (the One Led by God) to establish the kingdom of righteousness on earth. Afterward comes the end of the world. The Shiites believe that if the Twelfth Imam were not a living presence, the world would cease to be. They draw their spiritual strength from their faith in the Awaited One, they live and die for that faith. This is the simple human longing of a wronged, suffering community that finds hope and, above all, its sense of life, in that idea. We do not know when that Awaited One will appear; it could happen at any moment, even today. Then the tears will cease and each will take his seat at the table of plenty.

The Awaited One is the only leader the Shiites are willing to submit themselves to totally. To a lesser degree they acknowledge their religious helmsmen, the ayatollahs, and to a still lesser degree, the Shah. Because the Awaited One is the Adored, the focus of a cult, the Shah can be at best the Tolerated One.

From the time of the Safavids a dual authority, of the monarchy and the mosque, has existed in Iran. The relations between these two forces have varied but have never been overly friendly. If something disturbs this balance of forces, however, if, as happened, the Shah tries to impose total authority (with, to boot, the help of foreign backers), then the people gather in the mosques and the fighting starts.

For Shiites, the mosque is far more than a place of worship. It is also a haven where they can weather a storm and even save their lives. It is a territory protected by immunity, where authority has no right to enter. It used to be the custom that if a rebel pursued by the police took refuge in a mosque, he was safe and could not be removed by force.

There are marked differences in the construction of a mosque and a Christian church. A church is a closed space, a place of prayer, meditation, and silence. If someone starts talking, others rebuke him. A mosque is different. Its largest component is an open courtyard where people can pray, walk, discuss, even hold meetings. An exuberant social and political life goes on there. The Iranian who has been harassed at work, who encounters only grumpy bureaucrats looking for bribes, who is everywhere spied on by the police, comes to the mosque to find balance and calm, to recover his dignity. Here no one hurries him or calls him names. Hierarchies disappear, all are equal, all are brothers, and — because the mosque is also a place of conversation and dialogue — a man can speak his mind, grumble, and listen to what others have to say. What a relief it is, how much everyone needs it. This is why, as the dictatorship turns the screws and an ever more oppressive silence clouds the street and workplaces, the mosque fills more and more with people and the hum of voices. Not all those who come here are fervent Muslims, not all are drawn by a sudden wave of devotion — they come because they want to breathe, because they want to feel like people. . . .

The Shiite also visits the mosque because it is always close, in the neighborhood, on the way to everywhere. Teheran contains a thousand mosques. The tourist's uninstructed eye spots only a few of the most impressive ones. But the majority of them, especially in the poorer neighborhoods, are modest buildings difficult to distinguish from the flimsily constructed little houses in which the underclass lives. Built of the same clay, they melt into the monotonous faces of the lanes, back alleys, and street corners, resulting in a working, intimate climate between the Shiite and his mosque. No need to make long treks, no need to get dressed up: The mosque is everyday life, life itself.

The first Shiites to reach Iran were city people, small merchants and craftsmen. They would enclose themselves in their ghettos, build mosques, and set up their market stands and little shops next door. Craftsmen opened workshops nearby. Because Muslims should wash before they pray, baths appeared as well. And because a Muslim likes to drink tea or coffee and have a bite to eat after praying, there were also restaurants and coffee shops close at hand. Thus comes into being that phenomenon of the Iranian cityscape, the bazaar — a colorful, crowded, noisy mystical-commercial-gustatory nexus. If someone says, "I'm going to the bazaar," he does not necessarily mean that he needs his shopping bag. You go to the bazaar to pray, to meet friends, to do business, to sit in a café. You can go there to catch up on gossip and take part in an opposition rally. Without having to run all over town, the Shiite finds in one place, the bazaar, all that is indispensable for earthly existence and, through prayer and offerings, also ensures his eternal life.

V . S .   N A I P A U L

Islam in Malaysia and Indonesia

THE STORIES OF Joseph Conrad give an impression of the remoter places of the Malay Archipelago a hundred years ago: European coasting vessels, occasionally in competition with Arabs, men of pure faith; European trading or administrative settlements on the edge of the sea or the river, with the forest at their backs; Chinese peasants and laborers taking root wherever they can; Malay sultans and rajas, warriors with their courts; and, in the background, simpler Malays, people of river and forests, half Muslim, half animist.

Separate, colliding worlds: the world of Europeans, pushing on to the "outer edge of darkness," the closed tribal world of Malays: It was one of Conrad's themes.

V. S. NAIPAUL's portrait of Islam in Malaysia and Indonesia is from his 1981 classic Among the Believers: An Islamic Journey, which followed the lives of Muslims throughout the world. The author, also a noted novelist (A House for Mr. Biswas, A Bend in the River), was awarded the Nobel Prize in 2001.

And in Malaysia today the Islamic revolutionaries, the young men who reject, are the descendants of those people in the background, the people of river and forest. In Malaysia they have been the last to emerge; and they have emerged after the colonial cycle, after independence, after money.

There is now in Malaysia more than coconuts and rattan to be picked up at the landing stages. Malaysia produces many precious things: tin, rubber, palm oil, oil. Malaysia is rich. Money, going down, has created a whole educated generation of village people and drawn them into the civilization that once appeared to be only on the outer edge of darkness but is now universal.

These young people do not always like what they find. Some have studied abroad, done technical subjects; but not many of them really know where they have been. In Australia, England, or the United States they still look for the manners and customs of home; their time abroad sours them, throws them back more deeply into themselves. They cannot go back to the village. They are young, but the life of their childhood has changed.

And they also grow to understand that in the last hundred years, while they or their parents slept, their country — a new idea: a composite of kingdoms and sultanates — was colonially remade; that the rich Malaysia of today grows on colonial foundations and is a British-Chinese creation. The British developed the mines and the plantations. They brought in Chinese (the diligent, rootless peasants of a century back), and a lesser number of Indians, to do the work the Malays couldn't do. Now the British no longer rule. But the Malays are only half the population.

The Chinese have advanced; it is their energy and talent that keep the place going. The Chinese are shut out from political power. Malays rule; the country is officially Muslim, with Muslim personal laws; sexual relations between Muslims and non-Muslims are illegal, and there is a kind of prying religious police; legal discriminations against non-Muslims are outrageous. But the Malays who rule are established, or of old or royal families who crossed over into the new world some generations ago.

The new men of the village, who feel they have already lost so much, find their path blocked at every turn. Money, development, education have awakened them only to the knowledge that the world is not like their village, that the world is not their own. Their rage — the rage of pastoral people with limited skills, limited money, and a limited grasp of the world — is comprehensive. Now they have a weapon: Islam. It is their way of getting even with the world. It serves their grief, their feeling of inadequacy, their social rage, and racial hate.

This Islam is more than the old religion of their village. The Islam the missionaries bring is a religion of impending change and triumph; it comes as part of a world movement. In *Readings in Islam*, a local missionary magazine, it can be read that the West, in the eyes even of its philosophers, is eating itself up with it materialism and greed. The true believer, with his thoughts on the afterlife, lives for higher ideals. For a nonbeliever, with no faith in the afterlife, life is a round of pleasure.

"He spends the major part of his wealth on ostentatious living and demonstrates his pomp and show by wearing of silk and brocade and using vessels of gold and silver."

Silk, brocade, gold and silver? Can that truly be said in a city like Kuala Lumpur? But this is theology. It refers to a *hadith* or tradition about the Prophet. Hudhaifa one day asked for water and a Persian priest gave him water in a silver vessel. Hudhaifa rebuked the Persian; Hudhaifa had with his own ears heard the Prophet say that nonbelievers used gold and silver vessels and wore silk and brocade.

The new Islam comes like this, and to the new men of the village it comes as an alternative kind of learning and truth, full of scholarly apparatus. It is passion without a constructive program. The materialist world is to be pulled down first; the Islamic state will come later — as in Iran, as in Pakistan.

And the message that starts in Pakistan doesn't stop in Malaysia. It travels to Indonesia — 120 million people to Malaysia's 12 million, poorer, more heterogeneous, more fragile, with a recent history of pogroms and mass killings. There the new Islamic movement among the young is seen by its enemies as nihilism; they call it "the Malaysian disease." . . .

The statues of war and revolution in Jakarta were overemphatic; some were absurd. But they commemorated recent history; and that history was heroic and dreadful, and dizzying to read about.

It was the Japanese who, when they occupied Indonesia in 1942, abolished the Dutch language. They ordered all Dutch signs to be taken down or painted out; and overnight, after three hundred years, Dutch disappeared. The Japanese established Sukarno and other Indonesian nationalist leaders (imprisoned or exiled by the Dutch) in a kind of Indonesian government during the war. The Japanese organized the Indonesian army. This was the army that fought the Dutch for four years after the war, when the Dutch tried to reassert their rule. And this was the army that afterward, during the twenty years of Sukarno's presidency, held the scattered islands of the archipelago together, putting down Muslim and Christian separatist movements in various places.

Independence was not easy for Indonesia. It didn't come as regeneration and five-year plans. It came as a series of little wars; it came as chaos, display, a continuation of Sukarno's nationalist rhetoric. Sukarno's glamor faded. The army's power grew. It was the army that eventually, in 1965, deposed Sukarno. The army claimed that the communists were planning, with Sukarno's passive support, to take over the country. And after the chaos and frustrations of independence, there was a terror then greater than anything the archipelago had known.

A hundred thousand people were arrested. There was a massacre of Chinese (resident in Indonesia for centuries, and traditional victims of pogroms: The Dutch themselves killed many thousands in Jakarta in 1740). And it is said that in popular uprisings all over the archipelago half a million people thought to be communists were hunted down and killed. Some people say a million. Indonesians are still stunned by the events of 1965 and later. When they talk of 1965 they are like people looking from a distance, at a mysterious part of themselves.

Now the army rules. The khaki-colored army buses are everywhere; and Jakarta is dotted with the barracks of *kommando* units (strange, that this particular Dutch word should be retained) that fly the red-and-white Indonesian national flag. The army has made itself into a political organization, and it has decreed that it shall be powerfully represented in every government.

It is the army that holds the archipelago together. And army rule — after the Sukarno years of drift and rhetoric — has given Indonesian fifteen years of rest. In this period, with the help of Indonesian oil, Jakarta has sprouted its skyscrapers; the main roads have been paved; the beginnings of services appropriate to a big city have appeared. In this period of rest there has also grown up an educated generation, the first generation in fifty years to know stability. But the army rule chafes. And already — the trap of countries like Indonesia — with stability and growth there is restlessness.

The restlessness is expressed by the new Islam, the Islam that more than ritual, that speaks of the injustices done to Allah's creatures and of the satanic ways of worldly governments: the Islam that makes people withdraw, the more violently to leap forward.

It is dizzying to read of recent Indonesian history. And to look at it in the life of one man is to wonder how, with so little to hold on to in the way of law or country, anyone could withstand so many assaults on his personality.

Suryadi was in his mid-fifties. He was small, dark-brown, frail-looking. He was born in East Java and he described himself as one of the "statistical Muslims" of Indonesia. He had received no religious training; such religion as he had was what was in the air around him. He wasn't sure whether he believed in the afterlife; and he didn't know that that belief was fundamental to the Muslim faith.

He belonged to the nobility, but in Java that meant only that he was not of the peasantry. The Dutch ruled Java through the old feudal courts of the country. But Java was only an agricultural colony, and the skills required of the nobility in the Dutch time were not high. Suryadi's grandfather, as a noble, had had a modest white-collar job; Suryadi's father was a bookkeeper in a bank.

It was possible for Suryadi, as a noble, to go to a Dutch school. The fees were low; and Suryadi, in fact, didn't have to pay. The education was good. Just how good it was was shown by the excellent English Suryadi spoke. And recently, wishing to take up German again and enrolling in the German cultural center in Jakarta, the Goethe Institute, Suryadi found that, with his Dutch-taught German of forty years before, he was put in the middle class, and he was later able without trouble to get a certificate in an examination marked in Germany.

Early in 1942 the Japanese occupied Java. The message from Radio Tokyo was that the Japanese would give Indonesia its independence, and there were many people willing to welcome the Japanese as liberators. Suryadi was in the final year of his school. The Dutch teachers were replaced by Indonesians, and the headmaster or supervisor was Japanese. For six months classes continued as they would have done under the Dutch. Then — and it is amazing how things go on, even during an upheaval — Suryadi went to the university. The lecturers and professors were now Japanese. But the Japanese simply couldn't manage foreign languages. They recognized this themselves, and after time they appointed Indonesians, who worked under Japanese supervisors.

The Indonesians used the classes to preach nationalism. Already much of the good will toward the Japanese had gone. It was clear to Suryadi that the whole economy was being subverted to assist the Japanese war effort. Thousands of Indonesians were sent to work on the Burma Railway (and there is still a community of Indonesians in Thailand, from the enforced migration of that time). Radios were sealed; the radios that had once brought the good news from Radio Tokyo could no longer be listened to.

Two incidents occurred at this time which made Suryadi declare his opposition to the Japanese. The university authorities decreed that all students were to shave their heads. It was the discipline of the Zen monastery. And Suryadi felt it as he was meant to feel it: an assault on his personality. And then one day on the parade ground — students were given military training — a student was slapped by a Japanese officer. All the Indonesians felt humiliated, and Suryadi and his friends held a protest demonstration in the university. Thirty of them, teachers as well as students, were arrested by the Japanese secret police and taken to jail.

In the jail they heard people being tortured for anti-Japanese offenses and even for listening to the radio. But Suryadi's group were treated like political prisoners; and they continued to be disciplined in the way of the Zen monastery. They were beaten with bamboo staves, but it was only a ritual humiliation. The bamboo staves were split at the end; they didn't hurt; they only made a loud cracking noise. After a month of this Suryadi and his friends were released. But they were expelled from the university. So Suryadi never completed his education.

They had got off lightly because the Indonesian nationalist leaders were still cooperating with the Japanese. Sukarno never believed that Japan was going to lose the war, Suryadi said: Sukarno didn't even believe that the atom bomb had been dropped on Japan. It was only after the Japanese surrender that Sukarno and the nationalists proclaimed the independence of Indonesia. And four years of fighting against the Dutch followed.

What events to have lived through, in one's first twenty-six years. But Suryadi was without rancor. The events had been too big; there was no one to blame. He had no ill-feeling toward either Dutch or Japanese. He did business now with both; and he respected both as people who honored a bargain. The Japanese had the reputation in Southeast Asia of being hard bargainers (there had been anti-Japanese riots in Jakarta because of the Japanese domination of the Indonesian market); but Suryadi had found the Japanese more generous, if anything, than the Dutch.

Suryadi was without rancor, and it could be said that he had won through. But there was an Indonesian sadness in him, and it was the sadness of a man who felt he had been left alone, and was now — after the Dutch time, the Japanese time, the four years of the war against the Dutch, the twenty years of Sukarno — without a cause. More than once the world has seemed about to open out for him as an Indonesian, but then had closed up again.

He had lain low during the later Sukarno years. Army rule after that had appeared to revive the country. But now something else was happening. A kind of Javanese culture was being asserted. Suryadi was Javanese; the Javanese dance and the Javanese epics and puppet plays were part of his being. But he felt that Javanese culture was being misused; it was encouraging a revival of feudal attitudes, with the army taking the place of the old courts. Suryadi had the Javanese eye for feudal courtesies. He saw that nowadays the soldier's salute to an officer was more than an army salute; it also contained a feudal bow. It was a twisted kind of retrogression. It wasn't what Suraydi had wanted for his country.

And he had lost his daughter. She had become a convert to the new Muslim cause — the Malaysian disease, some people called it here. At school and then at the university she had been a lively girl. She had done Javanese dancing; she was a diver; she liked to go camping. But then, at the university, she had met a new Muslim, a born-again Muslim; and she had begun to change. She went out with her hair covered; she wore drab long gowns; and her mind began correspondingly to dull.

Suryadi and his wife had done the unforgivable one day. They had gone among the girl's papers, and they had come upon a pledge she had signed. She had pledged to be ruled in everything by a particular Muslim teacher; he was to be her guide to paradise. She, who would have been a statistical

Muslim like Suryadi and his wife, was now being instructed in the pure faith.

Suryadi didn't take it well. He thought now he should have been calmer in the beginning; by making his dismay too apparent he had probably pushed the girl further away from him. He said to her one day, "Suppose someone asks you to go out camping now, will you say, 'I cant' go, because I have no assurance there will be water for my ablutions before my prayers?'" He had spoken with irritation and irony. But later she came back to him and said, "I have checked. In the Qur'an there is nothing that says it is obligatory if you are traveling." And Suryadi understood then that she had become impervious to irony; that she had become removed from the allusive family way of talking. The intellectual loss was what grieved him most. He said, "But don't you have a mind any longer? Do you have to go to that book every time? Can't you think for yourself now?" She said, "The Qur'an is the source of all wisdom and virtue in the world."

She married the born-again Muslim who had led her to the faith. She had a degree; he was still only a student at the university; but, like a good Muslim wife, she subordinated herself to him. That was the new sadness that Suryadi was learning to live with: a once-lively daughter who had gone strange.

Still, recently he had found a little cause for hope. He was driving her back one day to her in-law's house, where she lived with her husband. He said, "I have bought that little house for you. Why don't you go and live there? Why does your husband want to keep on living with his parents? It isn't right. Why doesn't he make up his mind to act on his own?" She had said then, "He's got an inferiority complex, Father."

And this little sign, the first for some time, that his daughter still had a mind, was still capable of judging, was a great comfort to Suryadi.

She had seen what was clear to Suryadi: that the boy was a poor student, didn't have the background, couldn't cope with university life. He was still some way from taking his degree and wasn't giving enough time to his work. During the month of Ramadan, the fasting month, he had given up his work altogether, fasting all day and going to the mosque in the evening to pray. That was easier than being with the difficult books, and his religious correctness was admired by his Islamic group at the university.

Suryadi's daughter had seen this on her own. That was some weeks ago. And it was now what Suryadi was waiting for: that in time she might see a little more.

At the end, just before we separated, Suryadi said, "But I've been lucky. I haven't been like so many others in Indonesia, switching another wavelength under pressure."

"Another wavelength?"

"You know how people are like here. But perhaps you don't. They turn mystical. Logical, rational people. They start burning incense sitting up at night in graveyards if they want to achieve something. If they feel they are frustrated, not advancing in their work or career."

"Do you call that mystical?"

"I don't know what else you can call it."

Islam was the formal faith of the people. But below that were the impulses of the older world, relics of the Hindu-Buddhist-animist past, but no longer part of a system. The ninth-century temples of Borobudur and Prambanam— the first Buddhist, the second Hindu — were a cause for pride. But they were no longer fully possessed by the people, because they were no longer fully understood. Their meaning, once overpowering, now had to elucidated by scholars; and Borobudur remained a mystery, the subject of academic strife. It was the Dutch who rediscovered Borobudur and presented it to the people of Java: That was how Gunawan Mohammed, a poet and editor, put it. Gunawan — a Muslim, but in his own way, Indonesian way — said, speaking of the past and making a small chopping gesture, "Somewhere the cord was cut."

They were a people to whom the past was at once living and dead. And — whether they were talking about the killings of 1965 or about sitting up at night in a graveyard — they talked as though they remained mysterious to themselves.

And now, with the army peace, with the growth of industry and learning, with the coming to Indonesia of the new technological civilization, the world had grown stranger. I walked one Saturday evening in the market area of central Jakarta, the Pasar Baru, the New Bazaar, with the broken pavements, the mud, the shops full of imported goods, the food stalls, the amplified records. In this atmosphere of the fairground I came upon a bookshop. It was a well-lit shop and it had books on two floors. There were books in English on technical subjects — medicine, psychology, engineering. There was also a large section of English books on mystical or occult subjects — Taoism, *I Ching*, Paul Brunton's searches in secret India and secret Egypt. This was how the new civilization appeared: technical skill and magic, a civilization without its core.

After the dizzying history of the last fifty years, the world had grown strange, and people floated. Whether they moved forward, into the new civilization, or backward, like Suryadi's daughter, toward the purer Arab faith, they were now always entering somebody else's world, and getting further from themselves.

GENEIVE ABDO

Islam in Egypt

THE SCENE FROM my balcony, in one of Cairo's wealthiest districts, offered a view the world had somehow failed to notice. Each Friday, within minutes of the awe-inspiring refrain of *Allahu Akbar*, God is Great, dozens of men flocked to a small plaza below, each clinging to a green prayer mat. They laid them out in unison, turning a small triangle in the street into a sea of green — the color of the Prophet Muhammad. They removed their shoes and prostrated themselves toward the mosque and, far beyond, toward Mecca itself. I was intrigued not by the sound of the *muezzin*, whose eloquent echo can be heard in various keys across most Muslim cities five times a day, nor by the instant field of green, which I soon learned was commonplace wher-

GENEIVE ABDO's No God but God *(published in 2000) profiled previously inaccessible segments of Egyptian society. The result was a fascinating portrait of Islam in a volatile country. This excerpt examines the roots of Islamic faith in Egypt.*

107

ever Cairo's faithful gathered to pray. Rather, I was struck by the fact that the worshipers hunched over their mats were not the kind of men commonly seen in the street and coffee-houses of Cairo. One glance revealed their social class: The smooth feet of this well-groomed set stood in sharp contrast to the rough calluses many Egyptian men develop from dragging their bare heels over the edges of their ill-fitting shoes.

I was stunned that middle- and upper-middle-class men would leave their luxurious apartments and villas in Zamalek, once home to Egypt's pashas and kings, to pray on a dusty corner of Ahmed Hishmat Street. Nearly everything I had read before coming to Egypt in 1993 described the Islamic revival as a movement reserved for the poor. The common explanation in press accounts and academic circles for Egypt's return to its Islamic identity had become a cliché: After experimenting with socialism, Arab nationalism, and capitalism under successive leaders Gamal Abd al-Nasser, Anwar Sadat, and Hosni Mubarak, a vast majority of Egyptians were left poverty-stricken and embittered toward the West. The failures of Western-oriented ideologies and economic development, went the argument, fueled a rejectionist movement — hence, the nostalgic search for Islamic "roots."

But as I watched the men dressed in imitation Pierre Cardin sweaters and fine starched cotton shirts sprawled out along the green mats in the street, that theory rang false. In the months that followed, I met wealthy women from Dokki, another upper-crust district, who followed the teaching of a conservative *sheikh*, known for bringing wayward actresses and wives of government ministers back into the Islamic fold. After attending his religious lessons and listening to his Friday sermons at the local mosque, women who were once slaves to fashion took the veil and gave their expensive French wine to the secular friends they left behind. Instead of preparing lunch for their husbands in the mid-afternoon when the workday ends, they fasted and prayed, provoking tensions within their families.

There were ample outward signs that religion was penetrating nearly every sector of society. At Cairo University, a campus that is representative of middle-class Egyptian society, a majority of female students were veiled. And no matter where I went at noontime, whether it was a bank, an athletic club, the central telephone office, the grand bazaar downtown, or even the government press center, all business stopped for prayer.

The overwhelming Islamic sentiment on display begged an obvious question: What effect, beyond the symbols of veils and prayer mats, was the Islamic revival having on the spirit and values of ordinary people. I found my first clues in the two or three taxi drivers I met each day I roamed the city. The behavior of the drivers, who were always male and most of the time no older than forty, followed either one of two predictable patterns. If I heard cassettes on the tape player of popular *sheikhs* or religious music, if the drivers were dressed in a *gallabiyya*, the Islamic tunic, I felt at ease. Unlike those who played Egyptian pop music, attached photographs of bikini-clad women to their dashboards, contorted their necks to stare at my legs as I sat in the back seat, or adjusted their mirrors to fix their eyes on my face, hoping the unmanned steering wheel would find safe passage through the chaotic traffic, the men of religion were interested only in driving. When I heard the Qur'an playing as I hopped in a cab, I knew I would not be peppered with questions Egyptian men typically toss at foreign women: Was I married, did I have children, would I go on a date? I also knew a reasonable fare would suffice. There would be no haggling over money.

Thus began my search for the underlying causes of the Islamic revival in Egypt. It was clear from the beginning that the "economic determinist" theory, redolent of nineteenth-century European philosophy and so readily accepted in the West, particularly in the United States, did not hold up. Egyptians were clearly more concerned with bringing about social reform than they were with establishing economic equilibrium between the rich minority and impoverished majority. The Islamic revival was broad-based, touching Egyptians in every social class and all walks of life. All you had to do was look at the feet of the faithful on Ahmed Hishmat Street.

Two potent factors have allowed this revival to proceed largely unnoticed. It has been obscured on the one hand by the West's need to cast Egypt as a "democratic" and "secular" outpost in a bewildering and hostile Arab sea, and on the other by the distraction of Islamic militant groups waging a persistent, but ultimately ineffective, twenty-year challenge to the state. The 1979 Iranian revolution and the bloody struggles under way in Algeria, in Afghanistan, and, to a lesser extent, in southern Lebanon, have left a lasting impression on the Western consciousness of what to expect from the "Islamic threat." For a time, Egypt's own militants, led by the *al-Gama'a al-Islamiyya*, did their best to fulfill these expectations and reinforce Western stereotypes. From the late 1970's to the mid-1990's, militants killed dozens of foreign tourists, bombed banks, tour buses, an a café in a five-star Cairo hotel, assassinated cabinet ministers, attempted to kill president Mubarak himself, and carried out the bloodiest massacre in modern Egyptian history in the Pharaonic town of Luxor, in November 1997. Fifty-eight foreign tourists and four Egyptian were killed, some hacked to death with knives.

Generally, however, the militant movement inside Egypt has largely succumbed to the tenacity of the state security forces, the enmity of ordinary pious Egyptians, and the poverty of its own proclaimed ideology. Groups such as *al-Gama'a al-Islamiyya*, which emerged from the student protest movement in universities in the late 1970s, now find few supporters today on college campuses. Their leaders, the ideologues who vowed after the 1981 assassination of President Sadat to overthrow the secular state, have been killed by security forces, thrown in jail, or forced to flee abroad.

In place of the militant threat, a new type of Islamic revival, untested in the casbah of Algiers, the mountains of Afghanistan, and the back alleys of Tehran, has quietly taken shape and poses a far more significant challenge to Western interests in the Middle East. Egypt's "Popular Islam," a grassroots movement emerging from the streets, aims to transform the social structure of Egyptian society from the bottom up, creating an Islamic order.

Leading institutions, once under complete government control, have begun eroding the state's secularist policies. Universities, the courts, the official religious caste, or *ulama*, and in fact much of the middle class, including doctors, lawyers, and engineers, have created their own avenues to apply religious values in society. Students have kept political and religious activities alive on campuses, despite a state ban, by organizing underground Islamic-oriented groups and unions. Middle-class professionals developed a syndicate movement that offered hundreds of thousands of doctors, lawyers, and engineers a system of social services and an Islamic way of life independent from the state. Likewise, the *ulama* at al-Azhar, a thousand-year-old institution of Islamic learning, have shed their historical role as henchmen for the state and have challenged government policies on social issues ranging from female circumcision to birth control. They have asserted themselves as the moral and political guardians of Egyptian society. In doing so, they have extended their authority beyond the strictly religious sphere to ban books and films that they deem offensive to Islam and the Muslim community of believers.

The judicial system has also fallen under Islamic influence. In recent years, the courts have banned from cinemas films that were considered blasphemous to Islam. A film directed by Yussef Chahine, Egypt's most famous film-maker, was withdrawn after years of legal wrangling, with one court instructing the parliament to issue a law banning the depiction on screen or stage of the lives of Islamic holy figures. The ruling argued that while existing Egyptian law was ambiguous on the matter, religious law, the *sharia*, was not. Perhaps the most celebrated case involved a university professor who was declared an apostate for his writings about Islam. A court agreed with the charge against him and ordered the professor to divorce his wife, citing a law that a non-Muslim is prohibited from marriage to a Muslim woman. In both cases, the judges set what secularists regard as dangerous precedents. They exceeded their civil authority by interpreting religious texts, an exercise generally reserved for Islamic scholars.

The current religious revival has evolved from three waves of Islamic activism in Egypt, beginning in the nineteenth century. At that time, Jamal Eddin al-Afghani and his disciple, Mohammed Abdu, argued that Islam was a rational religion and should be interpreted in ways that could be applied directly to modern life. They believed tradition-bound Muslim leaders had led society astray, and that religious thinking should instead be reformed and used as a vehicle for progress. Their movement emerged in response to foreign intervention in Egypt, first through the Napoleonic invasion and later through British colonialism. Afghani and Abdu viewed the West as both a rival and a model, and offered a formula for Muslims that would incorporate some aspects of foreign culture and achievements while adjusting Islam to compete with the advances made in the non-Muslims world.

A second phase of Islamic revivalism occurred in Egypt in the early part of the twentieth century with the emergence of the Muslim Brotherhood. Founded in 1928 by Hasan al-Banna, it is still the Middle East's most venerable such group. Unlike the ideologues and theorists Afghani and Abdu, al-Banna aimed to apply religion directly to politics and popular life. A special apparatus was created within the Brotherhood to fight the British in Egypt and the Jews in Palestine. The Brotherhood's strategy was based on proselytizing and spreading the word through *al-dawa*, the Islamic call. It sought to gain political power, if necessary, by force. The Brotherhood became increasingly radical during the 1940s and 1950s. It demanded that women wear the veil, and ruled that nightclubs, cinemas, and theaters were sacrilegious and must be closed. Committed to the scriptures of Islam, to an Islamic social and political identity, and to the adaptation of religious principles to the demands of the modern world, the Brotherhood sought to reform Egyptians values, the economy, and the political system in order to create a Muslim society.

For a time it seemed that the Brotherhood would take control in Egypt, but the group was eclipsed by the Free Officer's coup in 1952, which brought Gamal Abd al-Nasser to power. Ideologically, Nasser's regime aimed to satisfy the desires and needs of society through a secular, rather than a religious, approach. With the Soviet Union as his financial patron and sometime ideological model, Nasser sought to establish a state based on socialist principles that would address the economic needs of people. Through policies based in pan-Arab nationalism and state domination of the economy, he held out the promise of social mobility through education and economic development.

Nasser banned the Muslim Brotherhood and imprisoned

hundreds of its members in the largest crackdown to date on the Islamic movement. To neutralize public criticism, he also co-opted members of the *ulama*, the official religious caste, to certify the policies of his government as "Islamic social-ism." Nasser drew a clear separation between religious and social matters, which he largely ignored, and political and economic reform, which he promoted, resting his legitimacy on his ability to improve the standard of living for the aver-age Egyptian. With the subsequent failure of his economic policies, society at large began shifting its focus back to reli-gion, and Nasser's credentials as a ruler of a Muslim country were called into question.

In 1967, Egypt's disastrous war with Israel was enough to expose the major social and ideological fault lines in Nass-er's Egypt. When the Israeli military humiliated the Egypt-ian army, the country entered into a period of soul-searching and began to question the principles upon which its national identity was based. There were no foreign powers to inflict defeat, no imperialists depriving the masses of the economic gains they were promised under the veil of Arab socialism. Egyptians had only themselves to blame. It was natural then for the country to seek to reestablish its national collective identity as a way to heal its wounds. That identity was Islam, summed up in the absolute profession of faith: There is no God but God, and Muhammad is His Prophet.

The third wave of Islamic activism, beginning in the 1970's and still under way, benefited greatly from the expe-rience of the previous decades. The Islamists leading the revival were more organized and methodical than their predecessors had been. By the end of the decade, the movement had split into those who advocated the creation of an Islamic society by peaceful means, and those who believed force was the only method by which to overthrow the government and establish an Islamic state. The moderates joined the Muslim Brotherhood, which by that time had renounced violence, and focused their efforts within the universities. They took over student unions that were once controlled by leftists, organized a network of religious activities, ranging from summer camps to meetings in mosques and dormitories, and provided affordable textbooks and religious literature on campuses. The radicals, meanwhile, carried out their first in a series of violent attacks in 1977, when militants kidnapped and then killed Egypt's minister of religious endowments. By 1981, the militants had gained enough organizational strength to assassinate President Anwar Sadat.

With radicals operating along the fringes, the moderate Islamists set about building widespread support within the broader society. Unlike the period of Afghani, and later, Hasan al-Banna and the early days of his Muslim Brotherhood, contemporary Islam has penetrated deeply into the Egyptian consciousness. Now, there is a widespread feeling that the cause of society's malaise stems primarily from a betrayal from within, rather than a domineering force from without. Here lies the greatest difference between the past and current revivals: Islamic thought in the late 1800s, and again in the 1940s and 1950s, focused on anti-imperialist sentiment and socioeconomic concerns, while the contemporary Islamic fervor emphasized family values, traditional sexual mores, and cultural authenticity.

This new focus is reflected in a change in the players leading the revival. Where society once looked to those with prophetic zeal, such as al-Banna, to lead them along the Islamic path, today's revival is more evenly diffused throughout Egyptian society. It relies neither on one man, nor one group, nor one institution. At the center of this new religious milieu, a powerful alliance of *sheikhs*, informal street preachers, scholars, doctors, lawyers, and women is groping its way toward a new, Islamic order. Today, the middle class, not what remains of the upper-class cultural elite, is defining social and religious norms. This broad base in turn supports a potent social movement that represents a formidable challenge to the secular state.

Contemporary Islamic movements can be plotted on a scale between revolutionary Iran, in which violent insurrection overthrew a secular regime and replaced it from the top down with an Islamic republic, and quietist Egypt, in which social reform is leading toward the Islamization of society at large from the bottom up. To date, the revolutionary path has left little lasting mark on the Arab world. The Iranian revolution, once regarded as a model for Islamic renewal, lost its credibility in the eyes of Muslim Arabs when the ayatollahs fell into internal power struggles and became bogged down by economic crisis and isolation from much of the Western world. Similarly, the Arab world's moderate Islamists have dismissed insurrections in Algeria and Afghanistan as being un-Islamic for the brutal and savage tactics adopted by the leaders of the

Islamic Group in Algeria and the Taliban in Kabul.

Egypt stands alone today for the progress it has made along this second path, characterized by moderate Islamists challenging state policies, rather than the state itself. Followers of radical Islamic movements maintain that living a fully integrated religious life will only be possible if their rulers govern by the word and law of God. Moderate Islamists in Egypt, however, are willing to live with a mixture of man-made laws and Qur'anic law, the *sharia*, which, according to Egypt's constitution, should be the "primary" source of legislation but in reality is not strictly applied. The flexible nature of Egypt's revival stands to make a profound contribution to the development of Islamic movements in the twenty-first century and will chart a new course for other countries to emulate in much the same way that the Iranian revolution captured the imagination of the Muslim world twenty years ago.

The Egyptian experience reflects centuries-old conflicts and contradictions among Sunni Muslims over the idea and role of the state. According to religious doctrine, the state was a divine institution responsible for carrying out God's intentions. However, the state was also perceived as a source of evil, and the less the citizenry had to do with it the better. The division of labor between the caliphs and the sultans came down to distinguishing between two kinds of authority, one prophetic and the other monarchical, but both religious. In modern terms, the struggle under way in Egypt among moderate Islamists is how to make state policy coincide with religious doctrine laid out by the *ulama* at al-Azhar and the thousands of independent and unlicensed *sheikhs*.

Egypt's nonviolent approach to integrating a modern state with God's laws reflects the historical influences of the country's earliest political culture and, later, its relationship to Islam after the Muslim Arab conquests of the seventh century. Egyptians under the rule of the Pharaoh had few individual rights. They were not allowed to question the form and nature of the state. Unlike the Greeks, they were excluded from participation in the political process; they could not debate, discuss, or oppose government. The Pharaoh's divine status placed him above the law; all functions of government were religious, not civil. The ruler's divine nature meant that obeying him and the laws he imposed was an act of faith. As a result, society was divided between believers and nonbelievers, not between citizens and noncitizens. This political experience wherein the citizenry survived by avoiding or ignoring, rather than confronting, an alien state has existed since time immemorial.

The Arab invasion of the seventh century shaped Egypt's character as an Islamic and Arabic-speaking nation, and for centuries loyalty to Islam was supreme over devotion to the state. For three centuries, between 1250 and 1520, Egypt was the center of religious activity in the Arabic-speaking part of the Islamic world. It remained the focus of spiritual and intellectual life until the Ottoman conquest, when Istanbul replaced Cairo as the center of religious authority.

Egypt's relationship with its new Muslim rulers was consistent with its history. Once Egyptians embraced Islam, Muslim leaders were no more interested in the welfare of the citizenry than their pagan predecessors had been. Until the nineteenth century, Egyptians identified with Islam on a broad scale, independent of their ruler, and tended to their economic needs on a community and personal level. Under Ottoman rule, the hierarchy of the religious establishment, the *ulama*, stepped in to offer religious guidance through their interpretation of religious texts, even when they had no influence on the rule of law in the state. Lower religious functionaries, such as the leaders of prayer and religious teachers in the countryside, led the faithful and helped establish a traditional, religious society independent from the state.

The political culture of Egypt has prompted some historians to conclude that revolution on a massive scale, whether politically or religiously motivated, is alien to the country's experience. Even when Egyptians were ruled for centuries by foreigners, from Alexander the Great in 332 B.C. to the fall of the last monarch, King Faruq, in 1952, they rebelled infrequently against their alien oppressors. Thus, the submissiveness and docility often associated with Egyptian citizens in their relationship to the state is not new; it remains firmly entrenched in the Egyptian psychology. More to the point, out of need during periods of foreign rule and out of inertia during Muslim dominance, Egyptians learned to rely on themselves and institutions outside the state for religious interpretation and moral guidance. . . .

But how can a society, saddled with a secular regime since the Free Officer's coup in 1952, undergo such a profound transformation without violent upheaval?

The answer lies in the flexible and realistic approach of today's Islamists. The figures leading the revival have matured since their forefathers led a crusade to oust the British from Egypt, beginning in the 1930s. Today's Islamists do not reject modernity; instead, they are searching for ways to marry their religious value system with the contemporary needs of their adherents. They intend to achieve this goal through the application of the *sharia*. This demand is not new to Egypt; it has been the core of the Muslim Brotherhood's program since its inception in 1928. As a concession to the Islamic movement, the Egyptian parliament in 1980 passed an amendment to the constitution making the principles of the *sharia* the main source of legislation. But despite the change, the law of the Qur'an has yet to be enforced.

The founders of the Muslim Brotherhood at one time favored a rigid interpretation of *sharia*. But today's Islamic modernists, some of whom have left the Brotherhood, generally believe Islamic law should be adapted to contemporary society. Egypt's Islamists, for example, say that if they came to power they would not require all women to be veiled, nor would they advocate cutting off the hands of thieves as is done in Saudi Arabia, where a strict interpretation of *sharia* is enforced.

The ideas of Egypt's Islamists during the last half of this century stem from thinkers such as al-Banna and Sayyid Qutb, the Trotsky of the modern Islamic movement. Unlike al-Banna, who believed in creating an Islamic society within the existing Egyptian state, Qutb advocated transforming society through proselytization and militant jihad, or holy struggle. This harder line later helped inspire the militant offshoot of today's Islamic movement, which took Qutb at his word. But both thinkers took as the starting point of their philosophies the all-consuming nature of Islam, which unifies religion and politics, the state and society.

"Islam cannot fulfill its role except by taking concrete form in society, rather, in a nation, for many do not listen, especially in this age, to an abstract theory which is not seen materialized in a living society," Qutb wrote in his landmark manifesto, *Milestones*. This volume stands alongside Lenin's *What Is to Be Done?* as a classic of the revolutionary genre and remains widely read in Egypt despite an official ban.

Many of Egypt's Islamists say they now find Qutb's ideas too radical and out of step with the times. Still, his books, as well as those of al-Banna, are eagerly consumed among university students, and serve as symbols of political resistance. At the very least, the ideas of Qutb and al-Banna have had an indirect influence on today's religious revival. Both men argued, for example, that Westernization of Muslim society and Western models for modernization should be rejected because they had failed the Muslim world and were responsible for political corruption, economic decline, social injustice, and spiritual malaise. This theme has clearly struck a chord with Egypt's professional classes, traditional engines of Western modernity, now turning against what they see as a flawed value system that undermines family and social bonds.

The power of such thinking, and its potential to mobilize political and social protest, should not be underestimated. In fact, similar sentiments provided significant impetus, particularly among disaffected intellectuals, for the 1979 Iranian Revolution, the greatest upheaval in this century carried out in the name Islam. The Iranian intellectual Jalal Al-e Ahmad could just as easily have been referring to Egypt when he warned of "the fundamental contradiction between the traditional social structures of the Iranians and all that is dragging our country toward colonial status, in the name of progress and development but in fact as a result of political and economic subordination to Europe and America." Writing in the 1960s, Al-e Ahmad went on to identify what he called the disease of *gharbzadegi*, often translated as "occidentosis" or "Westoxication." The term, refined and popularized a decade later, became a permanent fixture of the Iranian, and later the global, vocabulary of Islamic dissent.

In Egypt, the deep penetration of Muslim sentiment beyond state control first emerged during Sadat's presidency, in the late 1970's. This religious revival expressed itself in many ways; increased attendance at the mosque; the broad adoption of Islamic dress by men and women; a proliferation of religious literature and taped cassettes; and a burgeoning of Islamic organizations. Sadat encouraged the Islamic movement in universities to counter socialist and leftist holdovers from the Nasserite era opposing his government, until it became evident a decade later that the militant strand of the revival could no longer be contained.

Declared an apostate for making peace with Israel and condemned for aligning Egypt too closely with the United States, Sadat was assassinated by the same Islamic radicals he had helped strengthen a decade earlier. Sadat's assassins denounced his government as illegitimate primarily because it did not enforce religious law, and they determined the only solution was direct, armed confrontation. The assassins heralded the murder as a great Islamic victory over an infidel ruler. "I have killed Pharaoh and I do not fear death," proclaimed the lead gunman as he sprayed the president with automatic rifle fire.

The assassination inspired the militant groups, and the *Gama'a al-Islamiyya* turned its fire on cabinet ministers, foreign tourists, prominent intellectuals, and President Mubarak himself. But by the time the militant movement reached its apogee in the early 1990s, ordinary Egyptians had come to reject the radicals who killed in the name of religion. As the masses embraced Islam and a renewed value system, they became more and more alienated from the militant movement and more determined to tell whomever would listen that their religion had little to do with violence. In a rare opinion poll conducted at the end of 1994, by *al-Ahram* weekly, an English-language newspaper, 86 percent of Egyptians surveyed declared that Islamic groups that resort to violence do not work to the benefit of the country. Conversely, 73 percent of the respondents said nonviolent Muslim groups did benefit society.

The populist Islamic revival indeed charted its own course, free of violence and coercive tactics. According to government estimates, four thousand new mosques were constructed by the early 1980's, at least one thousand of which were erected through private initiatives, outside state supervision. Religious programming on state radio and television exploded, with both moderate and radical *sheikhs* spreading their message more effectively than ever. Qur'anic and religious schools mushroomed, and Islamic mystical orders increased fourfold.

President Mubarak's government has responded to the populist-led Islamic revival by conveying a conflicted message that is overreactive and tolerant, aggressive and compliant, often at the same time. The Islamic resurgence has made significant gains as a result of this schizophrenic policy toward religion. On the one hand, Mubarark's government has brutally attacked the militant trend, arresting thousands of suspected radicals, some of whom were tortured in prison and held for years without charge, according to human rights lawyers. The state has also imprisoned on minor charges moderate Islamists who never engaged in violence and tried to choke off informal channels feeding popular Islam, such as closing unlicensed mosques and banning unorthodox preachers from the pulpit.

Yet, like his predecessors, Mubarak has also sought to accommodate the Islamic tendency and earn a religious seal of approval. Like them, he is paying an increasingly steep political price, as a changing society pulls the president and the rest of the secularist ruling elite along in its wake. Firebrand preachers, for example, now spread their word on state-run television programs, and the government has turned a blind eye to members of the *ulama* at al-Azhar who have effectively replaced state censors as arbiters of which books and films violate accepted social values. In the spring of 1998, the Minister of Higher Education banned a textbook being used in a course at the American University in Cairo, a bastion of Egypt's secular elite. The book, a biography of the prophet Muhammad written by a renowned Marxist, was outlawed twenty-four hours after Islamists complained in state-run newspapers. There was no review of its political content, and no discussion concerning the book's role in providing intellectual balance in the course. The ban was issued immediately to prevent a scandal that would certainly spark anti-American rhetoric and raise questions over why the state would allow such a Western-style institution to exist on Egyptian soil.

Although state repression has led to victory over militant groups trying to overthrow the government, this same policy also produced a backlash within society and helped feed the nonviolent Islamic revival. The state's fatal flaw lies in its inability to distinguish the militant, who seeks its violent overthrow, from the peaceful Islamist, who seeks accommodation. By 1994, the rhetoric unleashed by authorities had one message: "All Muslim activists are terrorists." The tough talk soon became deed as thousands of students in universities across the country were arrested for participating in peaceful activities in the name of their religion. Dozens of Islamic engineers, lawyers, and doctors were also imprisoned after they swept to victory in professional union elections. As Egyptian students and the professional classes watched their nonviolent peers arrested for peaceful protest, they became increasingly determined to challenge the state's Islamic credentials. The state was winning the battle against the militants, but it was simultaneously losing the support of the common man and forcing society to create autonomous institutions through which to express its religious loyalties.

Mubarak's regime has clung to power by closing down all avenues of political participation. The Islamists have been banned from forming political parties, and impeded from election as independents through widespread fraud and vote rigging, according to Egyptian and international human rights organizations. The professional unions, of which they took control in free and fair elections, have been placed under state guardianship and effectively closed. But while the political process is not within the Islamists's reach at the moment, the social transformation of Egyptian society continues unabated with or without accommodation from the regime. . . .

The national struggle under way in Egypt cannot be simplistically classified as a clash between "Jihad" and "McWorld," as the scholar Benjamin R. Barber has described the confrontation he sees between Islam and modernity. Instead, the goal is marriage between the two. When Islamist leaders in Egypt's medical union, which represents hundreds of thousands of middle-class professionals, designed a health insurance program for its members, they used an American model. But they adapted it to fit their moral and religious beliefs. "Our insurance is American and Islamic at the same time," the architect of the program told me. "It's American because we have instituted a payment system for those who suffer from terminal diseases, such as cancer. It is Islamic because we never cut off the payments, no matter what happens. We keep paying until the patients are either cured or dead."

ROBERT D. KAPLAN

Islam in
Turkey

IN THE SECOND HALF of the eleventh century A.D. the first wave of Turkish nomads from
Central Asia arrived in Anatolia. They were
called Seljuks, after their founding chieftain.
Konya, the capital of this medieval Seljuk state,
was my first destination.

The Seljuks were fixated on the color that the French call
turquoise, which they may have seen first in the cratered lakes
that punctuated the desert plateau
on their journey to Anatolia from
Central Asia. In Konya, the flut-
ed, rocket-shaped dome covered
in luscious turquoise tiles above
the tomb of Cellaledin Rumi, the
preeminent religious mystic of the
Seljuk era, represents the ultimate in Seljuk architecture. The
fourteenth-century dome seems

ROBERT D. KAPLAN*'s*
profile of Islam in Turkey
is taken from his 1996
book, The Ends of
the Earth, *which*
profiled Third World
countries, including
a tolerant Islam
community in Turkey.
Kaplan, an acclaimed
foreign correspondent,
is also the author
of Balkan Ghosts.

to levitate above the surrounding cupolas and walls, like a hal-
lucination with height and width but no physical depth. This
dome supplies the sense of mystical awe that religions desperately require yet rarely attain.

Along with a throng of pilgrims, I removed my shoes and
entered Rumi's blue-domed mausoleum. A sign in English
greets visitors with Rumi's words "Come, come whoever you
are, whether you be fire worshipers, idolaters, or pagans.
Ours is not the dwelling place of despair. All who enter will
receive a welcome here." Turkish women wrapped in red
head shawls and men with beards and woolen hats mingled
easily with Western tourists amid the overlapping Oriental
carpets and gold-leafed qur'anic calligraphy framed by colorful tiles. Not just the tourists, but the pilgrims too, were happily snapping photos. Rarely had I been in a holy place with
such a welcoming climate. "Islam in other countries is often
based on fear of God. This breeds despotism, since fear of
God implies fear of authority. But Turks, due to the influence
of Rumi and other mystics, are moved by love of God, which
breeds tolerance," a former Turkish prime minister, Bulent
Ecevit, had told me in Ankara.

Actually, Rumi wrote in Persian. Persian literature and
architecture had a great influence on the Seljuks. It may be
telling that Rumi was a cult figure among hippies in the 1960s
and 1970s. He was born in 1207 in Balkh, in the northern,
Turkic, part of Afghanistan. As a boy, he traveled with his
father for several years across Persia and eastern Anatolia to
Konya (the hippie route to India, in reverse). Travel, evidently,
leavened Rumi's spirit, and his tolerance. A flower child of his

time, he believed that men, regardless of race or religion, were united, and linked to all of nature by love. This view, which may have had roots in the pre-Islamic past, was expressed in Rumi's characteristically sensuous poetry:

And I am a flame dancing in love's fire,
That flickering light in the depths of desire.
Wouldst thou know the pain that severance breeds,
Listen then to the strain of the reed.

Rumi believed that love of God transcends particular religions and nationalities and that Muslims are by no means the only people to whom God has revealed himself. Rumi said that we should simply say "farewell" to the "immature fanatics" who scorn music and poetry. He cautioned that a beard or a mustache is no sign of wisdom — if anything, travel (the nomadic life) will bring wisdom. Rumi was an ascetic, the opposite of a religious activist like Muhammad: He thought that men and women should shun politics and concentrate on discoveries of their inner selves. He favored the individual over the crowd and spoke often against tyranny, whether of the majority or of the minority. When Rumi died in Konya on December 17, 1273, Christians, Jews, Arabs, and Turks poured forth from the surrounding countryside to mourn. They cried en masse and tore their clothes as a sign of grief. His tomb became a site of pilgrimage. In a part of the world associated with fanatics, he is one of history's truly ecumenical figures.

Rumi helped define *Sufism*, a word that comes from the

Arabic *suf*, or wool. According to a qur'anic *hadith*, a man who wears wool lacks an ego. While submerging the ego through mystical dances and other practices, Sufism nevertheless emphasizes the importance of the individual, making some Turkish Sufi orders the most liberated of Muslim groups. They dance, occasionally drink wine, and admit women to membership, though not really as equals. One Sufi group, the Bektashis, supported Ataturk's secular nationalist movement, though some Sufi orders have worked against Ataturk's secularizing trend. Turgut Ozal, Turkey's late president and prime minister [from 1989 to 1993], was a devout Sufi. Ozal's deep religious commitment, combined with his intense dislike of Muslim dictators such as Iran's Ayatollah Khomeini and Iraq's Saddam Hussein, would have warmed Rumi's heart. Turkey's political future will be, in part, determined by how Sufism evolves. That evolution, in turn, will be influenced by urbanization — the pressures brought upon individual Turks as they fight to maintain their traditions in big cities, particularly in the *gecekondus*.

On April 22, 1993, the day that Turgut Ozal was buried in Istanbul, I knelt on the carpets in the mosque next to Rumi's tomb and talked with Ali Erhun, a twenty-eight-year-old religious official. He wore a white skullcap and a polite expression, and held prayer beads in his hand.

Erhun began by apologizing. He could not offer me the traditional cup of tea that Turks sip throughout the day from countless small glasses, because it was forbidden inside a mosque. Hospitality is a trait that Turks ascribe to their nomadic past, when survival depended on offers of kindness from strangers. But this kind of hospitality has another side: It sets very high standards for friendship, meaning it is easy for the West to fall short. That was the theme of Erhun's talk:

> "My family is descended from the Oghuz Turks, who migrated into Anatolia from Central Asia and captured Anatolia from the Byzantines. I was born in Cumali Koyu, not far from Istanbul. Here the first Ottomans arrived and needed a place to wash before praying. An old Sufi, someone like Rumi, pointed out a water source with his staff. Underneath that spot they found water. There they built the town. . . .
>
> "Central Asia is the country of our grandfathers. The end of Russia's domination in Central Asia means the eventual reunification of what used to be whole — Turkestan, the Turkic world. . . .
>
> "Turget Ozal, *may peace be upon him*, prepared us for this great transitional moment. Ozal softened the secular edge of Kemalism so that religious Turks now feel included in the system. This new freedom allows Turks to unite the present and future with the old cultures of the past, Seljuk and Ottoman. Islam is a serious component in this process."

But Erhun warned that the Western orientation of the Moslem Turks, nourished by Rumi's openness, was being eroded by the West's "desertion" of besieged Muslims in the Balkans and the Caucasus. As Erhun spoke against the oppression of Muslims, bearded men with skullcaps, who had gathered in the small anteroom of the mosque to hear our conversion, nodded their heads in agreement. The fighting in the Balkans and the Caucasus had suddenly riddled the atmosphere with tension.

"You, the West, are only a fair-weather friend." The prayer beads snapped through Erhun's fingers, but his voice remained calm:

"As hard as we try to be like you, you have always alienated us. Before helping the Catholic Croats and the Orthodox Serbs, you were on the side of the Greeks in Cyprus. You are forcing us to look eastward, toward the Turkic world, but only so much. We will continue to cooperate with America and Europe when it suits us. We will be a big player."

Erhun's eyes did not blink. He was ready for his final point.

"Islam was born in Arabia. The Arab's, for a long time carried the banner of the Prophet. But Arab civilization was not strong enough for this. So the Turks took over. For a thousand years, since our Seljuk ancestors defeated the Byzantine Greeks, we have carried the flag of Islam with honor. Konya, the Seljuk capital, is where we sit now. The *Mevlana* ["Teacher," a reference to Rumi] is buried a few feet from us. After the collapse of the Ottoman empire, the Arabs again picked up the Prophet's banner. But this was temporary. We, the Turks, are ready again for this role. Don't assume that just because Arabic is the language of the Prophet and of the Qur'an the Arabs will lead Muslims in this world. We too can lead Muslims. Our Islam, because of the *Mevlana*, is different from that practiced in Egypt and Saudi Arabia."

WILLIAM T. VOLLMANN

Islam in Afghanistan

ESCENDING THE KHYBER Pass
from Pakistan, one enters a tan-colored
desert that resembles the tough interior
membrane of a pomegranate — a weary-
ing, lifeless place. Emerald wheat fields,
trees shining with figs and oranges, and armies of snowy
hills present themselves from time to time, but the region is
mostly sand, pebble heaps, and drum-hard earth, tramped
down by glaciers and soldiers. I
remember gazing into that
desert from Pakistan, back in
1982. The Afghan insurgents I
was travelling with had shown
me a Soviet sentry box and the
road behind it that went on into
infinity. It was a reasonably
good road then. By the time I
returned, last January, hardly a

WILLIAM T. VOLLMANN
*is a metafictional
novelist and journalist,
who explores the
harrowing lives of the
world's underclasses.
In May 2000, Vollmann
traveled through a
devastated Afghanistan
to find out more about
the country's leaders.
This essay first appeared
as a much longer piece
in* The New Yorker.

scrap of asphalt remained on its bomb-cratered, potholed track.

I had never driven down it before. In 1982, my companions had led me over the mountains from the Pakistani town of Parachinar in order to avoid the Soviet garrison. Now this border crossing was open. After eighteen years, I was going back to a country that had been my symbol of heroism — a place where poor peasants had risen up against arrogant and cruel invaders and washed them away with their own blood. Those invaders had been gone for a decade. The new government, run by members of the fundamentalist Islamic movement known as the Taliban, was literal-minded and stern, like the freedom fighters who'd inspired me years before. It was despised by much of the Western world, but I wanted to know what the Afghans, who had to live with it, thought.

My translator and I changed money in the border town of Torkham, got a taxi, and rattled down into Afghanistan. For scenic attractions, we had the stumps of a razed orange grove, wrecked Soviet tanks, and refugee mud villages, abandoned now and crumbling into dust. There were warnings of land mines, and once in a great while a listless-looking man could be seen far off on the dreary plain, dragging a golf-club-shaped mine detector through the rocks. I saw virtually no usable habitation, not even a tent. Nevertheless, every few hundred yards there'd be a dirty boy or girl waiting by the side of the road. As our taxi approached, the child would sink a shovel just far enough into the dirt to collect a few clods, then dribble them into the nearest pothole, pretending to improve the road for our journey, hoping for payment. A burning stare, a shout, and then we were on our way to the next beggar.

If I stopped and gave money to a child, others came running. I slipped one boy five thousand afghanis — about ten cents — and when I looked back in the rearview mirror it seemed that the other boys were practically tearing him to pieces. On a road bend where no other beggar could see, I gave a twenty-dollar bill to a boy who stood beside the carapace of a Soviet armored personnel carrier, and he took it and held it as if he were dreaming. I wanted him to hide it before anybody else came or the wind took it from him, but the last I saw of him he was still standing there with the banknote dangling from his hand.

It was like this most of the way to Kabul, some hundred and twenty miles from the border. Inside the capital's war-pocked walls, beggar women and children would wait outside the windows of restaurants, crowding against the glass and drumming on it desperately. If I sent a plateful of food out to them, they'd fall on it in the same way that skates and manta rays occlude their scavenged prey — guarding it with their own flesh while they eat. When I left the restaurant and got into a taxi, the children would try to climb in, too. I couldn't bring myself to slam the door on their hands, so the taxi would roll down the street with the door open, gradually increasing speed until they had to let go. Once I went out alone at dusk, and an army of children fell upon me, clawing at me for money, shouting obscenities, and laughing that the Taliban would kill me because I wore bluejeans instead of the stipulated shalwar kameez — a long shirt and baggy pantaloons.

They were the children first of war and then of poverty, growing up hungry and ignorant (although some of the boys claimed to go to school), with not much either to amuse them or to make them hopeful.

But I must have been missing the point: In Pakistan, where I'd spent almost three weeks waiting for an Afghan visa, people had rhapsodized about the quality of life in Afghanistan. Several Afghan women teachers I met in a refugee camp expressed admiration for the Taliban — even though under Taliban rule they wouldn't be allowed to teach. A Pakistani government official in Islamabad said that he adored the Talibs. And in the border city of Peshawar, where I stayed in a six-dollar hotel, the clerk, a gentle, bad-complexioned boy, who came to my room every evening to answer questions about the Qur'an, told me, "Afghanistan is now the most perfect country in the world." Times had changed. In 1982, every Pakistani male I met had wanted to be photographed. But although this boy trusted me, he refused to let me take his picture, because the Taliban had decreed that doing so broke the rules of Islam.

The Volunteers

IN AFGHANISTAN'S DESERTS, plains, and valleys live many ethnic groups — the Pashtuns, the Tajiks, the Hazaras, and others — who greet strangers with a welcoming hand on their hearts and devote themselves with equal zeal to blood feuds. The mountains stand sentinel between them, and each group tends to keep to itself. Thanks to

Islam, each sex likewise keeps itself apart from the other. So Afghans live both separately and inwardly, whether they sleep in tents or wall themselves away in fortresses of baked mud. They are watchful, hospitable, yet withdrawn, magnificent and vindictive, kind and lethally factional, untiringly violent. In the fierce stewardship of their honor, Afghans sometimes remind me, despite their religious differences, of the Serbs. But, unlike the Serbs, they are repelled by the concept of nationality. Each group tells its own stories — the Caucasian-looking Pashtuns bad-mouthing the Asiatic-looking Hazaras, and vice versa — and "government" operates in a distant dreamland where houses have electricity, women can read, and officials flaunt the money they've extorted from the people. What unites the Afghans, if anything, is the monitory, glorious religion of Islam.

It follows, then, that those who do not pray, or who pray to other gods, must stay forever beyond the pale, while those who believe as the Muslim does, no matter what their color, language, or nationality, are his brothers and sisters. This is why Muslim zealots call for a worldwide Islamic state, and why the Iran-Iraq War was infinitely more distressing to Muslims than any conflict between two Christian nations would be to us in our easy secularity. (So ingrained is this notion of Muslim kinship that the very few secret Christians of Afghanistan, who risk imprisonment to hold clandestine Bible readings at home, unfailingly embraced me and called me "brother.") Therefore, when the Soviet Union invaded Afghanistan, in December 1979, fighters came at once from Saudi Arabia, and, to varying degrees, from Pakistan,

Yemen, Libya, Tajikistan, and other Muslim regions. There may have been some thirty-five thousand of these nominally foreign volunteers.

Afghanistan had been far from stable before the invasion. The long-standing Afghan monarchy had been overthrown in 1973, in a military coup led by a cousin of the king, Muhammad Daoud. Then, after five years in power, Daoud and seventeen members of his family were killed by pro-Soviet Afghan leftists, who planned to achieve their own form of utopia by forcibly de-Islamicizing the countryside. By the time the first Russian troops arrived, a year later, those Communist Afghans had been largely discredited among the masses, who resented their atheism and cruel vanguardism.

Ironically, the Soviet invasion did much to unite Afghanistan. The country's many tribes and factions banded together to proclaim a jihad, or religious war, against the Soviet infidels. And the United States helped to arm these insurgents. In those days, they were "freedom fighters" to us, not "terrorists." They called themselves mujahideen, or holy warriors, but to the C.I.A. the religious aspect of the jihad was irrelevant — the war was "strategic," a good way to get back at the opposing chess team in Moscow.

When I went to Afghanistan in 1982, I supported the struggle in every way that I could, because it seemed one of the clearest cases I had witnessed of good versus evil. The mujahideen were certainly not guiltless then, but the deeds of the Soviets were unspeakable. They raped women in the name of emancipating them. In the defense of national security, they machine-gunned illiterate peasants who couldn't have found Moscow on a map. They burned people alive and drowned them in excrement. They razed villages, slaughtered livestock, and destroyed harvests. They even scattered mines disguised as toys, to lure people to their own maiming. In 1982, I saw several of these mines lying, unexploded, on the ground. Between a million and two million Afghans were killed in that war, 90 percent of them civilians. (Of the more than six hundred thousand Soviet soldiers sent to Afghanistan, fewer than fifteen thousand were killed.) The Afghans I met at that time were bright-eyed with fervor. Sick refugees said, "Tell America not to send medicine. Send guns." In the secret insurgent base where I stayed, not far from the Pakistani border, a commander told me, "I am not fighting for myself or even for Afghanistan. I am fighting only for God."

On February 15, 1989, to the world's amazement, the Soviets marched out of Afghanistan. The Afghans had won the war! Within a few years, they had ousted the Russians' last show ruler, President Muhammad Najibullah, and installed in his place a white-bearded Islamic scholar named Burhannudin Rabanni. But, instead of putting war behind them, the mujahideen — who had now organized themselves into seven factions, constituted, in customary Afghan style, along geographical, tribal, and sectarian lines — trained their weapons on one another. Each camp struggled for supreme power in Kabul, some supported by puppetmasters in other countries — Iran, Pakistan, Saudi Arabia, and, perhaps, the United States — transforming the war for liberation into a bloody and protracted civil war.

With the factions locked in battle like fighting beetles in a jar, five years went by and, according to one estimate, twenty thousand people died. Then, in 1994, the residents of Kabul heard a rumor from the south. It seemed that a group of young men — Islamic students, or *taliban* — had risen up in Kandahar, Afghanistan's second-largest city, which was then proverbial for its lawlessness. In the name of Allah the Beneficent, these Taliban, as members of the movement came to be known, had slain, captured, or driven off every criminal. Then they had confiscated all weapons, promising that they themselves would provide protection for the citizens. The streets secured, they applied Islamic law as they saw fit: They banned photographs, education for girls, and music. They demanded that women cover their faces in the street and leave home only in the company of a close male relative. All men found themselves required to grow beards and could be sent to prison for ten days if they shaved. In keeping with the Qur'an, the Taliban amputated the right hands of thieves. Kandahar was now so safe, it was said, that anyone could leave a bar of gold in the street and it would be there three days later.

The origins of the movement are murky. It reportedly began with forty Talibs, but no one could tell me how quickly other Afghans decided to join them. Their leader, Mullah Muhammad Omar, who'd lost an eye in the jihad, was reputed to be a quiet, simple man, although it was also said that he enjoyed a legal complement of three wives, one of whom was rumored to be as beautiful as any princess in the Arabian Nights. The fact that almost nobody was allowed to meet him enhanced his mythic stature. Some claimed that Mullah Omar and his followers were soldiers of the old king, Zahir Shah, who'd been deposed more than two decades before and was now in exile in Italy. Others suspected that they might be fanatics who meant to take away what scant freedoms remained in Afghanistan. But they were not rapists or wanton murderers like the other fighters, and most Afghans, paralyzed by decades of war, withheld judgment, as the Taliban spread to other cities and provinces, calling upon each man in their path to lay down his weapons in the name of Allah. For the most part, they were received with respect, even love: They brought peace. "I was proud to give up my arms," a tea-shop proprietor I met told me. "I started my jihad for an Islamic Afghanistan, and so we succeeded." Every time the Taliban disarmed others, their own arsenal grew.

In a few places, however, they encountered significant opposition. It took the Taliban cadres several attempts to conquer the northern city of Mazar-i-Sharif, which was then occupied by a former mujahideen general. The first time, the Taliban were invited in and then betrayed, thousands of them killed in cold blood. Their second attempt to take the city was repulsed. The third succeeded, at which point the Taliban are said to have murdered a thousand civilians. (I heard this figure go as high as five thousand. In central Asia, as in every other part of the world, atrocity statistics are always suspect.) A Hazara former civil servant told me that after the massacre he had seen stray dogs eating human flesh in the streets, and stacks of corpses, "like piles of firewood."

The Taliban also encountered resistance in Kabul, which, when they arrived in 1995, was still under the control of President Rabanni and his most famous general, Ahmed Shah Masoud, a brave and brutal Tajik fighter. The resistance that Masoud mounted against the Talibs in Kabul, together with the city's perceived decadent cosmopolitanism, made the Taliban especially harsh on the people there, once they had won control.

Still, by 1998, the Taliban had conquered about 90 percent of Afghanistan. Despite their frequent attempts to complete the takeover — which are said to have caused as many as forty thousand casualties — the other 10 percent, a swath of land in the northeast of the country, remains under the control of Masoud, Rabbani, and their supporters, who call themselves the National Islamic United Front for the Salvation of Afghanistan, and are also known as the Northern Alliance.

Who are the Talibs who are running Afghanistan now? They are Muslims, only a little more so. At five-thirty every morning, they don black, white, or green turbans and go to the mosque like other Afghans. (The *muezzin*, whose beautifully quavering song calls everyone to prayer, is now most often a Talib.) They come home and read the Qur'an or the *hadiths* — the recorded sayings and doings of the Prophet Muhammad — until sunrise. Afterward, they take tea. They go to work. Some Taliban are shopkeepers. Some work at the Ministry for the Propagation of Virtue and the Prevention of Vice.

Fifteen minutes after I arrived in Kabul, I met one of these worthies (my translator, awed and anxious, warned me how powerful he was). He was walking down a snowy street, across from a park in which children were playing. Kabul is high and cold — a ruin surrounded by mountains — so poverty is more lethal there. Men struggle to support their families, selling their belongings for a little food. They lurk on corners, looking for buyers. When I greeted the Talib, he instantly invited me home for tea. His responsibility at the Ministry was to police the front lines for anti-Taliban sentiment and to ensure that all the soldiers wore beards and refrained from smoking opium. He also investigated cases of Talibs who misused the signature turban in order to extort money. He and three colleagues who shared his house — two young men, one shy older man — sat with me on the floor of a bleak concrete room. They treated me with the usual Afghan politeness — handshakes, the most comfortable cushion, hands on their hearts. Even when they learned my nationality, their courtesy did not flag.

Diplomatic relations between our countries were suspended in 1998, when the United States bombed bases in Afghanistan that it claimed were run by Osama bin Laden, a Saudi-born former mujahid, who United States officials believe was responsible for the 1998 bombings of American embassies in Tanzania and Kenya. Later, when the Taliban refused to hand bin Laden over to American justice, the United Nations imposed sanctions. Now most of the Afghans I met hated the United States, and they withdrew from me a little in dignified sadness, but they still, like these four Talibs, spoke with me and invited me into their homes.

The concrete walls of the Talibs' room displayed nothing but cracks; all emblems were prohibited. Even their Qur'ans were wrapped lovingly out of sight. When I unclothed mine, in order to ask them some textual questions, tears started in one man's eyes. They wanted to help me learn. A space heater waxed and waned, according to the vagaries of that day's electricity. As we sat and chatted, they scrupulously filled my tea glass. We passed the time. I asked how I might go about interviewing a woman, and they said that they could arrange a conversation through a black curtain, but once I pressed them they retreated, and after some discussion they concluded that to speak with any female I would first need to get permission from the Ministry of Foreign Affairs. I told them not to trouble themselves further in this matter, and their spirits lifted.

We talked about the jihad. All four had been mujahideen. The three younger men had spent their childhoods wandering in and out of Pakistan, as their families changed refugee camps according to the latest military reverse or factional split. When they were about ten years old, their fathers had enrolled them in *madrasahs*, or religious schools, the only remaining institutions of learning in the country. (This was, and is, the way to become a member of the Taliban.) There they were taught Islamic law without ambiguities: Cut off the thief's hand. The woman must cover herself. How much of herself must she cover? The Qur'an doesn't tell us exactly, so make her cover everything! Such an edict is easy to enforce. This is army life, and these boys were soldiers. Every summer, they would take up their Kalashnikovs and shoot at Soviet tanks or gunship helicopters. They were taught that if they fell in battle they'd go to Heaven. After the war, they returned to their religious studies, and, when they heard about the corruption of the former mujahideen and the emergence of the Taliban movement, they travelled to Kandahar to enlist.

"Were you feeling happy, or did you simply feel compelled to do your duty?" I asked the man who'd invited me to tea.

"So happy! We volunteered," he replied.

"What was the first thing you did in Kandahar?"

"We instituted Islamic law."

"And were the people pleased?"

"They gave us flowers and money."

Later, a little awkwardly, he pulled up the baggy cotton legs of his shalwar kameez and showed me the scars on his legs from fighting for the Taliban. He had spent a month in the hospital. Smiling, half proud, half ashamed, he gazed down at his wasted purple flesh.

On my innumerable trips between Peshawar and Islamabad to obtain an Afghan visa, I had travelled through the little Pakistani town of Akora Khattak, the site of the most famous *madrasah*, Darul Uloom Haqqania, where the three younger Talibs had studied. The madrasah stands right on the main road, and an armed guard lazes outside its high white walls. About 30 percent of the current Taliban leadership, including the Ambassador to Pakistan and the Foreign Minister, have passed through the school's spiked iron gate. The rank and file study there by the thousand.

The head of the school was in Libya on the day of my visit, so I met with his son, Rashid ul Haq, the editor-in-chief of the militant Islamic monthly *Al-Haq*. If anyone could help me understand the Taliban's interpretation of Islamic law, or Sharia, I thought, it was he. We sat on the carpet of an inner room, attended by bearded, shining-eyed men in prayer caps or turbans.

"What makes the Taliban government different from that of other Islamic states?" I asked.

"You have seen the other countries," ul Haq replied, "but the others are living not according to the Qur'an but according to their own choice."

"Why have the Taliban made beards compulsory for men?"

"All prophets have beards," he said. "So we want to have beards. Some of the people, you know, live their lives according to the *hadiths*."

I wondered if he knew how unpopular this edict had become. As slang for "I left Afghanistan," some Afghan men had begun to say "I shaved the beard." Surgeons especially hated the rule, because in their own compulsory beards dwelled their patients' worst enemies: microbes.

"And why is music forbidden?" I asked.

"Islam does not permit it. People who sing create the thing that causes cowardice. And when a person spends his time in singing he loses his time."

"And what about the prohibition on images of people and animals?"

"In the *hadiths*, the picture is forbidden for the man," ul Haq said, and later added, "but Islam allows it when there is a need, as for visa photographs and pictures on currency."

I had just interviewed two Afghan brothers in a nearby

refugee camp who loved the Taliban, except for one thing. Their father had been martyred in the jihad, and all they had to remember him by was a small photograph. They told me that if the Taliban ever found it they might tear the picture into pieces.

"And exactly why does Islam say that such pictures are forbidden?"

"We do not want to see the logic of this talk," one of the other Taliban interjected. "What the Qur'an says is right. The logic is present."

The Western notion that the Taliban imposed themselves by force on an unwilling population is less than half true. Six years after that first unexpected uprising against the bandits of Kandahar, when one might well expect the Afghans to be heartily sick of any regime in whose name their misery continued, many people I spoke with expressed contentment with the Taliban. Why? Quite simply, because they could not forget how bad it had been before.

Afghanistan was never rich. During the war with the Soviet Union, men used to fight over the scrap iron of Russian bomb casings even as other bombs fell upon them; one entrepreneur actually posted mujahideen slogans in the desert so that the Soviets would bomb them and he could collect the metal. And, by the time the Taliban marched onstage, the civil war had made matters worse.

In a long, thick-walled teahouse in the Abrishini Gorge, on the main road between Jalalabad and Kabul, I sat cross-legged on a concrete platform and ate oiled chicken and bread while a middle-aged former taxi-driver told me how it had been in that vacuum of years between the Soviets and the Taliban. Pointing down at the gray-green river, he said, "That was where they took my two passengers."

Back then, in this part of the country, ex-mujahideen gunmen had established roadblocks every kilometer or two, where they would extort money from the taxi-driver's passengers. One night, when the taxi-driver reached one of these roadblocks, the men gestured with their rifle butts and summoned two men from the back of his car. The driver watched them being frog-marched into the gorge, and then the gunmen told him that he could go. His remaining passengers urged him to resist, but he was terrified. Fortunately, the two kidnapped men were released, although, of course, they'd been stripped of their possessions. The driver never forgot his helpless fear and shame. That was why he revered the Taliban. Not a single one of those checkpoints remained in the Abrishini Gorge: Now Talibs sat tranquilly beside machine guns, gazing down at the road from their stone forts.

"You know how hard it is to take the weapon from Pashtun people," one Talib had said to me proudly. "Ninety percent of the Afghan people now live in weapon-free areas."

"If things keep getting safer," the former taxi-driver said, "I don't care about not being allowed to listen to the radio."

"My two sons were both martyred by Masoud," an old beggar woman in Kabul had told me — illegally, since it was against the law for her to talk to me. "One lay for forty-seven days in a well. My husband was also martyred when the Masoud people stole his car. Now I'm looking for food in the streets. At least the Taliban won't kill me."

"They are better than everyone," another beggar woman said.

How many Afghans truly felt as those women did? Predictably, when the happiness over the restoration of peace wore off and the poverty and hardship remained, some of the gratitude soured. On the street in Kabul, late one cold evening, I met an old night watchman with a long snowy beard. All five of his sons had died in the jihad, he told me. To lose five children — I can hardly even understand the grief, and one must understand it, or at least try, if one wants to come close to experiencing the terrible reality of Afghanistan's misfortunes. One must also consider the plight of the homeless orphans — there are so many of them — and of the hungry widows and the brideless boys. "I have given my children and my brothers for this country," the night watchman added. "Now look at me. I am doing this job for my food only, and it is very cold. What kind of life is this?"

His words were not quite an indictment of the Taliban. I've met many human-rights advocates who, exasperated with the regime's judicial and extrajudicial abuses, rushed to lay blame on Mullah Omar's cadres for everything else — the short life expectancy in Afghanistan, the extraordinarily high infant-mortality rate, and so on. The fact is that the Afghan countryside was always unclean and unhealthy; people have always died young. To me, it is indicative of the regime's popularity (or, in some cases, of the fear that it inspires) that more Afghans do not denounce its turbaned agents of perfection.

But some do. Whereas the jihad and the civil war had harmed the population almost indiscriminately, Taliban policy has created a smaller, more specific class of victims. More than two-thirds of Mullah Omar's cadres are Pashtuns, who make up about 55 percent of the general population, and several of the other ethnic groups feel a certain chill in the air. Some were victimized during the Taliban takeover. Many of the civilians killed by the Taliban in Mazar-i-Sharif, for instance, were Turkmen, Uzbeks, and Hazaras. Some are discriminated against by the Taliban for religious reasons; the Hazaras, who comprise about 8 percent of the population, tend to belong to the minority Shia sect of Islam, whereas most Pashtuns are Sunnis.

Women, particularly urban, educated women, have suffered some of the most painful consequences of the Taliban's interpretation of Islamic law. Many who had lost family members in the jihad or civil war then lost their jobs under the Taliban — along with their freedom of movement and dress — and now have no means of supporting themselves; most are forced to beg.

In the opinion of a Kabuli boy, who resented this strictness — he could not get enough work and was the sole source of money and food for the women in his family — 40 percent of the people support the Taliban now, but only 5 percent are true members.

"How can they keep control?" I asked.

"They have Kalashnikovs," he said.

Punishments and Other Stringincies

AGAIN AND AGAIN, I was faced with contradictions, with the question of how to balance the feelings of the people for whom the new regime was a welcome kind of peace against the rights of those for whom it was a form of oppression.

I remember a sallow boy who hated the Taliban and whispered hideous details of punishments he'd witnessed in the stadium at Mazar-i-Sharif: a thief's right hand severed with a scalpel (by a doctor; it took ten minutes); the shooting of murderers. He claimed to have seen about thirty executions over the last two years — not because he had to but only "to see something new." Without music or movies or magazines, one might as well go to watch the punishments. Once he had seen a couple stoned for adultery. "They were in one bed, and Taliban see them. First, judge begin with one stone, then all of the people hit them with stone. They cry — they cry! Very high cry."

"How long did it take?"

"I think for one hour or one and a half hours, maybe two hours." He went on, "It's too bad, in my opinion. I feel the Taliban are wild. Please, I never tell any other foreigner these things. You are my brother. Please, dear brother, you will not tell them what I say? Because they will cut off my head!"

He went to the door of his room to see if anybody might be listening. No one was.

"What do you think?" he asked me.

"I don't know what to think," I said. "I'm only a Christian.

Those punishments you speak of, they're all here in the Qur'an. What do you think?"

He took my Qur'an in his hands and began kissing it, agonized, whispering, "Qur'an is a very, very good book."

Afghans insist upon the Qur'an's absolute legitimacy in all walks of life — as an ethical guide, a primer on hygiene and food preparation, a marriage manual, a tax code, a dress code, a body of criminal law. In that last capacity, it clearly conflicts with several articles of the Universal Declaration of Human Rights, which Afghanistan signed in 1948. The stoning of adulterers presumably falls under the category of "cruel, inhuman, degrading treatment or punishment"; the constraints on relations between the sexes violate the declaration's "right to freedom of peaceful assembly and association"; and so on. But if a believing judge sentences a believing thief to lose his right hand it is none of my business.

There are times, however, when the Taliban rulers winnow from the *hadiths* the most punitive interpretations of Islam. In the Qur'an, we read over and over that the compassion of Allah forgives transgressions in emergencies. A man in Kabul, who had just served a prison sentence for having defied the prohibition on images, told me about a scene he had witnessed: A thief whose right hand had already been cut off had stolen again, and so the Taliban cut off his left foot. Afterward, when they were beating him in prison, he shouted, "If you cut everything off I will continue stealing with my teeth! *Because I have nothing to eat!*" Yet the punishment was still carried out. And why was it that the boy who told me those tales of public penalties enforced on legally convicted criminals found it necessary to scutter to the door every minute or two, terrified that someone might be listening?

"They misuse the Qur'an," the woman who had worked for Radio Kabul insisted. "In the Qur'an, it is not written that even for pilfering you must cut off the hand. No, the real meaning of that verse is metaphorically cutting the hand from robbery, for instance through imprisonment." Her argument is somewhat plausible; the Qur'an explicitly warns against literal interpretations. But I assume that the allegorical *suras* are not the laws. Otherwise, why not say that the requirement to pray five times a day or to keep Ramadan can be satisfied metaphorically?

I am not a Muslim; I have read the Qur'an only twice. I needed to question a Talib whose authority allowed him to take some responsibility for legal questions of right and wrong. The Minister of the Interior, Mullah Abdul Razzaq, was kind enough to see me without advance notice.

After being searched by Kalashnikov-adorned young cadres at the entrance to the Ministry building, I was conducted upstairs and through halls where Talibs flurried around my foreignness. When the interview was over, I gave a chocolate bar to the dirtiest, hungriest-looking one of them. He was wearing a T-shirt that said "Oakland Raiders." When I told him that the Oakland Raiders were American, he was crestfallen, and the others all laughed at him. He did not seem to know what the chocolate bar was, although I had bought it in Kabul, at one of the few fancy stores still in existence. He peeled off the foil wrapper with a filthy thumbnail, then stared at the chocolate in amazement, while the other

Talibs gathered around, crowding so tightly against me that I could hardly breathe.

In the inner offices, however, a glacial decorum reigned. Ten farmers involved in a land dispute sat silently around a stove, wrapped in blankets, while the official to whom they'd referred their case was seated at a low coffee table, his great desk swept clean behind him. Beyond them lay an unheated conference room, and then a sanctum with carpets, cushions, and a little bed, where perhaps the Minister of the Interior took catnaps when he had to work all night. I took off my shoes and sat down on the floor to wait for him.

Mullah Abdul Razzaq is said to have been one of the founders of the Taliban movement. Of course, he'd fought bravely in the jihad and attended the *madrasah*. He'd been captured by Dostam during one of the battles for Mazar-i-Sharif. I had heard that he could be very emotional, but he and his colleagues entered the room calmly. His turban was white, and his black beard was very long. The other Talibs in the room bowed and nodded when he spoke, and his hands gestured slowly, serenely, in his lap.

"Why did you decide to become a Talib?" I asked him.

"It is said in the Holy Qur'an that when there is crying and corruption the people should fight against that," he said.

"As Minister of the Interior, you are in charge of security. Who controls crime in the streets, the police or the Taliban?"

"We control the crime," he said. "We control every department."

"What is the most frequent crime against the Sharia?" I asked.

"The Taliban have full control," he replied. "Right now, there is no crime."

A police officer I met in Kabul, a twenty-seven-year veteran, had written a letter for me to smuggle to distant relatives in California, and he whispered that the Taliban had robbed the police of their power. Possibly he and his colleagues had been corrupt before, as is frequently the case in Third World countries where the salaries of officials are so low that their only hope for survival is graft. If so, then Taliban rule might have been a change for the better. On the other hand, one can easily imagine the impatiently righteous graduates of the *madrasahs* preferring lampposts to courtrooms. There had been highly publicized instances of this already: On the night that the Taliban entered Kabul, Afghanistan's former President, the pro-Soviet Najibullah, was plucked from the United Nations compound, in which he had been cowering, and was tortured, castrated, shot, then hanged outside the palace. A similar fate befell his brother. (I was told by a reliable source — the same person had informed me that Osama bin Laden had a kidney complaint a day before the international media picked up the story — that Razzaq had personally ordered these executions.) No Afghan I've met has ever lamented these two men, but the speed of their killing, which was carried out within a couple of hours of the Taliban's arrival, not to mention the absence of judge, jury, and other formalities, occasioned some brief international embarrassment.

"Is it true that the penalty for beardlessness is ten days in jail?" I asked Razzaq.

"Yes, that is true."

"And why not nine or seven days?"

"That is the job of the Department of Religion. Only security is our job."

"Why is a *burka* better than a chador?" I asked.

"A *burka* covers all, so it is the real thing for women."

Razzaq became glum at this mention of the Taliban's treatment of women, much as he did when I later raised the question of Osama bin Laden, and we moved briefly to other subjects. "Sir, do you have any special message for the Americans?"

"We fought against Russia for years, and the Americans helped us," Razzaq said. "And we ask them and their government to help us again. As Afghanistan is destroyed, we expect help in reconstruction, and facilities for widows and orphans."

The matter of widows and orphans had particularly weighed on me. I felt that the Taliban government had no Islamic justification in its treatment of them. Since Razzaq had brought the subject back around to women again, I asked him, "Who is helping those widows now?"

"The Minister of Religion has promised some programs. And also the N.G.O.s" — nongovernmental organizations, or charities — "have done something."

"Does Islam permit widows with no other resources to go out and beg?"

"We are trying our best to prohibit them from this, and we are trying to give them facilities."

"But if they have no such facilities, if they are hungry, is it permitted?"

"It is still prohibited."

A Glance from Across the Divide

THE MINISTER'S ANSWER gave the Taliban a pitiless public face indeed, scorning the needs of the literally faceless. In truth, though, this regulation did not seem to be enforced. The beggar women plied their trade quite openly, even when Taliban passed by.

Afghans are no less pragmatic than other people, and continued exposure over the years to the realities of government and society seemed to be helping these Taliban children of war to mature. Year by year, even in Kabul, the theocracy was growing more moderate. As the brave girl had told me, the behavior of the Taliban has been "affected by humans."

When the Taliban first came to Jalalabad, in September 1996, they searched house to house, for televisions, videocassettes, and other irreligious items. They used the confiscated televisions for target practice. They required stores to remove labels from shampoo bottles wherever a human face was shown. But this February a retired professor there told me that the searchers had quickly tired of their unpopular investigations. Originally, he said, they'd believed that all urban dwellers were corrupt, but now they'd begun to realize that most citizens were not so bad; or perhaps some of the Taliban were growing corrupt themselves. (The Talib who worked the reception desk of my guesthouse in Jalalabad kept hitting me up for film in a most un-Islamic manner.) The professor watched television every day now — an activity that, in 1996, would have meant a fifteen-day jail sentence. Now the Taliban would not bother to come to his home unless someone proffered eyewitness testimony against him, and even in such a case they would merely confiscate his television — and possibly keep it for themselves, he said, laughing. He felt safe, and pleased to have the Taliban in power. They didn't care anymore if women went out alone, he told me. (I myself had verified this: When I visited the Talib dignitary from the Ministry for the Propagation of Virtue and the Prevention of Vice, he had tried to persuade me that women didn't have it so bad in Afghanistan. At one point, he and his three friends had called out excitedly for me to come and look at the street. "Look, look! Do you see? A lady, and her face is not covered, and no one is caring!")

In Kabul, I discovered in store windows one or two soap labels that bore the likenesses of women. And there was even a photograph of people (with no faces showing) mounted on the door of a taxi. Outside the cities, my taxi-drivers always listened to music, lowering the volume when they approached Taliban checkpoints, but not troubling to turn the radio off. In Pakistan, I'd met a doctor who had emigrated when the Taliban banned the possession of anatomical diagrams. But a doctor who'd stayed told me that things were not so bad now. "Before, we saw them beating women in the street. Now for a long time I don't see these beatings anymore. And now we have a camera in my operating room, and even projectors. I'll tell you a story. One Talib brought his wife to me. I refused to treat her without a letter of authorization, because that is what they make everybody else do. So he brought his wife to Pakistan. And I think he started to wonder about this policy."

One United Nations official, speaking of the Afghans, told

me, "What they need is more outsiders, more exchange of ideas." Thanks to the United Nations, that is precisely what they aren't getting. The sanctions have begun their strangling work. Gasoline and wheat are smuggled in from Pakistan (and duty-free appliances and cars are smuggled from Dubai through Afghanistan and out to Pakistan), but the price of bread is rising in Kabul, and hungry families blame the Americans. An Afghan rug merchant told me, "First you created one Osama. Now you are creating many, many Osamas."

Americans worry that Afghanistan has become a petri dish in which the germs of Islamic fanaticism are replicating — soon Afghans will be hijacking American planes and bombing embassies everywhere. And their fears are not necessarily unfounded. The Taliban are unemployed war veterans, ready and even eager to return to the battlefield. "In the nineteenth century, we beat the British more than once," Afghans often told me. "In the twentieth century, we beat the Russians. In the twenty-first, if we have to, we'll beat the Americans!" Sarwar Hussaini, the director of a Peshawar-based human-rights organization called the Coöperation Centre for Afghanistan, told me that Afghanistan was full of terrorist-training camps, that Pakistanis, Chechens, Uzbeks, and Arabs were there, learning to fight for Islamic supremacy in their own countries.

But is Afghanistan the puppet-master or the puppet? Masoud is said to receive money from Russia and Iran. Pakistan, a patron of all seven factions during the jihad, is now closely allied with the Taliban. The Iranians have financed some Hazara groups in Afghanistan. China is also dabbling, for fear of Muslim power invading its own territory. And

Saudi Arabia has broken off diplomatic relations with the Taliban, and therefore is suspected of aiding either Masoud or Gulbuddin Hekmatyar, another former mujahid. The Afghans themselves blame neighbors and superpowers for everything that has befallen them.

The Taliban could have come to power in any war-torn Islamic country. They gained supremacy in Afghanistan because all other leaders and movements there had discredited themselves through selfishness, vanguardism, gangsterism, and, above all, factionalism. Barring further mischief on the part of the superpowers, the Taliban may defeat Masoud and win their civil war. And it's entirely possible that as rulers they are preferable to any of the competition.

"I think Afghan people should choose neither Taliban nor Masoud," Hussaini told me. "Masoud is not a good alternative — he's proved that by his corruption. And the Taliban are not the kind of people one should like." But whom should the Afghans choose instead? A few old-timers long for the King to come back, but most people just say flatly that no good leader exists. Should the Taliban fall apart, it seems likely that the political and educational vacuum in Afghanistan will remain.

In Kabul, I stood in a grimy, unheated bookstore, some of whose books had been Islamicized, the faces on the jackets blacked out with splotches of Magic Marker. The bookstore seemed to have been subjected to this process randomly, though, as if the morality police had got tired or wandered off to look for something to eat. In the corner stood a rack of postcards from before the war, the faces depicted on them untouched. Dusty travel posters of "exotic" tribesmen remained on the wall.

As I talked to the bookseller, three Talibs entered the store, with black turbans wrapped around their faces like coiled cobras. Slowly, with wide eyes, whispering each word, they began to sound out the titles of the books. Soon, another joined them, whether searching for vice or merely passing the time I didn't know, and neither did the bookseller, who hung his head in breathless silence. They were looking for something — they seemed suspicious and disapproving — but perhaps they doubted their ability to find what they sought. Or maybe they were just cold. We could all see our breath condensing.

With the frightened bookseller translating, I asked one of them to tell me his happiest and saddest memories, and he said, "In my twenty-eight years of life, there's been nothing but war. Of course I have never been happy."

"Not even when you took Kabul?"

"That one day," he conceded without interest.

The Taliban asked me where I was from, and when I told them they fixed me with looks of rage.

"Tell the Americans that we believe their government is responsible for all our problems, and that they must stop this terrorism against us," the leader said curtly.

But they meant well. What they really wanted to do was to invite me into Islam. I showed them my Qur'an, and, as all their comrades had, they took it eagerly into their hands, kissed it, and slowly and silently began reading from it, their lips moving in a rapture. They promised me that if I became a Muslim they would take care of me forever. They'd feed and shelter me for the rest of my life. They'd find a special teacher for me. I'd become their brother. They gazed at me from across the divide, waiting.

THE
CONFLICTS

K A R E N   A R M S T R O N G

Muslims and
the West

THE RISE OF the West is unparalleled in world history. The countries north of the Alps had for centuries been regarded as a backward region, which had attached itself to the Greco-Roman culture of the south and had, gradually, developed its own distinctive version of Christianity and its own form of agrarian culture. Western Europe lagged far behind the Christian empire of Byzantium, where the Roman Empire had not collapsed as it had in Europe. By the twelfth and thirteenth centuries these western European countries had just about caught up with the other core cultures, and by the sixteenth century had begun a process of major transformation that would enable the West to

KAREN ARMSTRONG *is one of the world's foremost scholars on the conflicts between Islam and the West. This excerpt, from* Islam: A Short History, *chronicles the origins of Islam and the jihad, or Holy War. Armstrong is the author of several best-selling books, including* The History of God *and* The Battle for God.

dominate the rest of the world. The achievement of such ascendancy by an outgroup is unique. It is similar to the emergence of the Arab Muslims as a major world power in the seventh and eighth centuries, but the Muslims had not achieved world hegemony, and had not developed a new kind of civilization, as Europe had begun to do in the sixteenth century. When the Ottomans had tried to reorganize their army along Western lines in the hope of containing the threat from Europe, their efforts were doomed because they were too superficial. To beat Europe at its own game, a conventional agrarian society would have to transform itself from top to bottom, and re-create its entire social, economic, educational, religious, spiritual, political, and intellectual structures. And it would have to do this very quickly, an impossible task, since it had taken the West almost three hundred years to achieve this development.

The new society of Europe and its American colonies had a different economic basis. Instead of relying upon a surplus of agricultural produce, it was founded on a technology and an investment of capital that enabled the West to reproduce its resources indefinitely, so that Western society was no longer subject to the same constraints as an agrarian culture. This major revolution in reality constituted a second Axial Age, which demanded a revolution of the established mores on several fronts at the same time: political, social, and intellectual. It had not been planned or thought out in advance, but had been the result of a complex process which had led to the creation of democratic, secular social structures. By the sixteenth century Europeans had achieved a scientific

revolution that gave them greater control over the environment than anybody had achieved before. There were new
inventions in medicine, navigation, agriculture, and industry. None of these was in itself decisive, but their cumulative
effect was radical. By 1600 innovations were occurring on
such a scale that progress seemed irreversible: a discovery in
one field would often lead to fresh insights in another.
Instead of seeing the world as governed by immutable laws,
Europeans had found that they could alter the course of
nature. Where the conservative society created by agrarian
culture had not been able to afford such change, people in
Europe and American were becoming more confident. They
were now prepared to invest and reinvest capital in the firm
expectation of continuing progress and the continuous
improvement of trade. By the time this technicalization of
society had resulted in the industrial revolution of the nineteenth century, Westerners felt such assurance that they no
longer looked back to the past for inspiration, as in the agrarian cultures and religions, but looked forward to the future.

The modernization of society involved social and intellectual change. The watchword was efficiency: An invention or
a polity had to be seen to work effectively. An increasing
number of people were needed to take part in the various scientific and industrial projects at quite humble levels — as
printers, clerks, factory workers — and in order to acquire a
modicum of the new standards, they had to receive some kind
of education. More people were needed to buy the mass-pro-
duced goods, so that to keep the economy going an increasing
number of people had to live above the subsistence level. As

more of the workers became literate, they demanded a greater share in the decisions of government. If a nation wanted to use all its human resources to enhance its productivity, it had to bring groups who had hitherto been segregated and marginalized, such as the Jews, into mainstream culture. Religious differences and spiritual ideals must not be allowed to impede the progress of society, and scientists, monarchs, and government officials insisted that they be free of ecclesiastical control. Thus the ideals of democracy, pluralism, toleration, human rights, and secularism were not simply beautiful ideals dreamed up by political scientists, but were, at least in part, dictated by the needs of the modern state. It was found that in order to be efficient and productive, a modern nation had to be organized on a secular, democratic basis. But it was also found that if societies did organize all their institutions according to the new rational and scientific norms, they became indomitable and the conventional agrarian states were no match for them.

This had fateful consequences for the Islamic world. The progressive nature of modern society and an industrialized economy meant that it had continuously to expand. New markets were needed, and, once the home countries had been saturated, they had to be sought abroad. The Western states therefore began, in various ways, to colonize the agrarian countries outside modern Europe in order to draw them into their commercial network. This too was a complex process. The colonized country provided raw materials for export, which were fed into European industry. In return, it received cheap manufactured Western goods, which meant that local industry was usually ruined. The colony also had to be transformed and modernized along European lines, its financial and commercial life rationalized and brought into the Western system, and at least some of the "natives" had to acquire some familiarity with the modern ideas and ethos.

This colonization was experienced by the agrarian colonies as invasive, disturbing, and alien. Modernization was inevitably superficial, since a process that had taken Europe three centuries had to be achieved at top speed. Where modern ideas had time to filter down gradually to all classes of society in Europe, in the colonies only a small number of people, who were members of the upper classes and — significantly — the military, could receive a Western education and appreciate the dynamic of modernity. The vast majority of the population was left perforce to rot in the old agrarian ethos. Society was divided, therefore, and increasingly neither side could understand the other. Those who had been left outside the modernizing process had the disturbing experience of watching their country become utterly strange, like a friend disfigured by disease and become unrecognizable. They were ruled by secular foreign law-codes which they could not understand. Their cities were transformed, as Western buildings "modernized" the towns, often leaving the "old city" as a museum piece, a tourist trap, and a relic of a superseded age. Western tourists have often felt disoriented and lost in the winding alleys and apparent chaos of an oriental city: They do not always appreciate that for many of the indigenous population, their modernized capitals are equally alien. People felt lost in their own countries.

Above all, local people of all classes of society resented the fact that they were no longer in control of their own destiny. They felt that they had severed all connection with their roots, and experience a sinking loss of identity. . . .

The colonial experience and the collision with Europe had dislocated Islamic society. The world had irrevocably changed. It was hard for Muslims to know how to respond to the West, because the challenge was unprecedented. If they were to participate as full partners in the modern world, Muslims had to incorporate these changes. In particular, the West had found it necessary to separate religion and politics in order to free government, science, and technology from the constraints of conservative religion. In Europe, nationalism had replaced the allegiance of faith, which had formerly enabled its societies to cohere. But this nineteenth-century experiment proved problematic. The nation states of Europe embarked on an arms race in 1870, which led ultimately to two world wars. Secular ideologies proved to be just as murderous as the old religious bigotry, as became clear in the Nazi Holocaust and the Soviet Gulag. The Enlightenment *philosophes* had believed that the more educated people became, the more rational and tolerant they would be. This hope proved to be as utopian as any of the old messianic fantasies. Finally, modern society was committed to democracy, and this had, in general, made life more just and equitable for more people in Europe and America. But the people of the West had had centuries to prepare for the democratic experiment. It would be a very different matter when modern parliamentary systems would be imposed upon societies that were still predominantly agrarian or imperfectly modernized, and where the vast majority of the population found modern political discourse incomprehensible.

Politics had never been central to the Christian religious experience. Jesus had, after all, said that his Kingdom was not of this world. For centuries, the Jews of Europe had refrained from political involvement as a matter of principle. But politics was no secondary issue for Muslims. We have seen that it had been the theater of their religious quest. Salvation did not mean redemption from sin, but the creation of a just society in which the individual could more easily make that existential surrender of his or her whole being that would bring fulfillment. The polity was therefore a matter of supreme importance, and throughout the twentieth century there has been one attempt after another to create a truly Islamic state. This has always been difficult. It was an aspiration that required a jihad, a struggle that could find no simple outcome.

The ideal of *tawhid* would seem to preclude the ideal of secularism, but in the past both Shiites and Sunnis has accepted a separation of religion and politics. Pragmatic politics is messy and often cruel; the ideal Muslim state is not a "given" that is simply applied, but it takes creative ingenuity and discipline to implement the egalitarian ideal of the Qur'an in the grim realities of political life. It is not true that Islam makes it impossible for Muslims to create a modern secular society, as Westerners sometimes imagine. But it is true that secularization has been very different in the Muslim world. In the West, it has usually been experienced as benign. In the early days, it was conceived by such philosophers as John Locke (1632–1704) as a new and better way of being religious, since it freed religion from coercive state control and enabled it to be more true to its spiritual ideals. But in the Muslim world, secularism has often consisted of a brutal attack upon religion and the religious.

Atatürk, for example, closed down all the *madrasahs*, suppressed the Sufi orders, and forced men and women to wear modern Western dress. Such coercion is always counterproductive. Islam in Turkey did not disappear, it simply went underground. Muhammad Ali had also despoiled the Egyptian *ulama*, appropriated their endowments, and deprived them of influence. Later Jamal Abd al-Nasser (1918–70) became for a time quite militantly anti-Islamic, and suppressed the Muslim Brotherhood. One of the Brothers, who belonged to the secret terrorist wing of the society, had made an attempt on al-Nasser's life, but the majority of the thousands of Brothers who languished for years in al-Nasser's concentration camps had done nothing more inflammatory that hand out leaflets or attend a meeting. In Iran, the Pahlavi monarchs were also ruthless in their secularism. Reza Shah Pahlavi (reigned 1921–41) deprived the *ulama* of their endowments, and replaced the Sharia with a civil system; he suppressed the Ashura celebrations in honor of Husain, and forbade Iranians to go on the Hajj. Islamic dress was prohibited, and Reza's soldiers used to tear off women's veils with their bayonets and rip them to pieces in the street. In 1935, when protesters peacefully demonstrated against the Dress Laws in the shrine of the Eighth Imam at Mashhad, the soldiers fired on the unarmed crowd and there were hundreds of casualties. The *ulama*, who had enjoyed unrivaled power in Iran, had to watch their influence crumble. But Ayatollah Muddaris, the cleric who attacked Reza in the parliamentary Assembly, was murdered by the regime in 1937 and the *ulama* became too frightened to make any further protest. Reza's son and successor, Muhammad Reza Shah (reigned 1944–79), proved to be just as hostile to and contemptuous of Islam. Hundreds of *madrasah* students who dared to protest against the regime were shot in the streets, *madrasahs* were closed, and leading *ulama* were tortured to death, imprisoned, and exiled. There was nothing democratic about this secular regime. SAVAK, the shah's secret police, imprisoned Iranians without trial, subjected them to torture and intimidation, and there was no possibility of truly representative government.

Nationalism, from which Europeans themselves had begun to retreat in the latter part of the twentieth century, was also problematic. The unity of the *ummah* had long been a treasured ideal; now the Muslim world was split into kingdoms and republics, whose borders were arbitrarily drawn up by the Western powers. It was not easy to build a national spirit, when Muslims had been accustomed to think of themselves as Ottoman citizens and members of the Dar al-Islam. Sometimes what passed as nationalism took a purely negative stance and became identified with the desire to get rid of the West. Some of the new nations had been so constructed that there was bound to be tension among their citizens. The southern part of the Sudan, for example, was largely Christian, while the north was Muslim. For a people who were accustomed to defining their identity in religious terms, it would be hard to establish a common "Sudanese" nationalism. The problem was even more acute in Lebanon, where the population was equally divided among at least three religious communities — Sunni, Shii, and Maronite Christian — which had always been autonomous before. Power sharing proved to be an impossibility. The demographic time bomb led to the civil was (1975–90), which tragically tore the country apart. In other countries, such as Syria, Egypt, or Iraq, nationalism would be adopted by an elite, but not by the more conservative masses. In Iran, the nationalism of the Pahlavis was directly hostile to Islam, since it tried to sever the country's connection with Shiism and based itself on the ancient Persian culture of pre-Islamic period.

Democracy also posed problems. The reformers who wanted to graft modernity on to an Islamic substructure pointed out that in itself the ideal of democracy was not inimical to Islam. Islamic law promoted the principles of *shurah* (consultation) and *ijmah*, where a law had to endorsed by the "consensus" of a representative portion of the *ummah*. The *rashidun* had been elected by a majority vote. All this was quite compatible with the democratic ideal. Part of the difficulty lay in the way that the West formulated democracy as "government of the people, by the people, and for the people." In Islam, it is God and not the people who gives a government legitimacy. This elevation of humanity could seem like idolatry (*shirk*), since it was usurpation of God's sovereignty. But it was not impossible for the Muslim countries to introduce representative forms of government without complying with the Western slogan. But the democratic ideal had often been tainted in practice. When the Iranians set up their Majlis (Assembly) after the Constitutional Revolution of 1906, the Russians helped the shah to close it down. Later, when the British were trying to make Iran a protectorate during 1920s, the Americans noted that they often rigged the elections to secure a result favorable to themselves. Later American support for the unpopular Muhammad Reza Shah, who not only closed down the Majlis to effect his modernization program, but systematically denied Iranians fundamental human rights that democracy was supposed to guarantee, made it seem that there was a double standard. The West proudly proclaimed democracy for its own people, but Muslims were expected to submit to cruel dictatorships. In Egypt there were seventeen general elections between 1923 and 1952, all of which were won by the popular Wafd party, but the Wafd were permitted to rule only five times. They were usually forced to stand down by either the British or by the king of Egypt.

It was, therefore, difficult for Muslims to set up a modern democratic nation-state, in which religion was relegated to the private sphere. Other solutions seemed little better. The Kingdom of Saudi Arabia, founded in 1932, was based on the Wahhabi ideal. The official view was that a constitution was unnecessary, since the government was based on a literal reading of the Qur'an. But the Qur'an contains very little legislation and it had always been found necessary in practice to supplement it with more complex jurisprudence. The Saudis proclaimed that they were the heirs of the pristine Islam of the Arabian peninsula, and the *ulama* granted the state legitimacy; in return the kings enforced conservative religious values. Women are shrouded from view and secluded (even though this had not been the case in the Prophet's time), gambling and alcohol are forbidden, and traditional punishments, such as the mutilation of thieves, are enshrined in the legal system. Most Muslim states and organizations do not consider that fidelity to the Qur'an requires these pre-modern penal practices. The Muslim Brotherhood, for example, from a very early date condemned the Saudis' use of Islamic punishments as inappropriate and archaic, especially when the lavish wealth of the ruling elite and the unequal distribution of wealth offended far more crucial qur'anic values.

Pakistan was another modern Islamic experiment. Muhammad Ali Jinnah (1876–1948), the founder of the state, was imbued with the modern secular ideal. Ever since the time of Aurengzebe, Muslims had felt unhappy and insecure in India: They had feared for their identity and felt anxious about the power of the Hindu majority. This naturally became more acute after the partition of the subcontinent by the British in 1947, when communal violence exploded on both sides and thousands of people lost their lives. Jinnah had wanted to create a political arena in which Muslims were not defined or limited by their religious identity. But what did it mean for a Muslim state which made great use of Islamic symbols to be "secular"? The Jamaat-i Islami, founded by Abul Ala Mawdudi (1903–79), pressed for a more strict application of Sharia norms, and in 1956 the constitution formally defined Pakistan as an Islamic Republic. This represented an aspiration, which now had to be incarnated in the political institutions of the country. The government of General Muhammad Ayub Khan (1958–69) was a typical example of the aggressive secularism that we have already considered. He nationalized the religious endowments (*awqaf*), placed restrictions on *madrasah* education, and promoted a purely secular legal system. His aim was to make Islam a civil religion, amenable to state control, but this led inevitably to tension with the Islamists and eventually to Khan's downfall.

During the 1970s, the Islamist forces became the main focus of opposition to the government, and the leftist, secularist Prime Minister Zulfaqir Ali Bhutto (1971–77) tried to mollify them by banning alcohol and gambling, but this was not sufficient and in July 1977 the devout Muslim Muhammad Zia al-Haqq led a successful coup, and established an ostensibly more Islamic regime. He reinstated traditional Muslim dress, and restored Islamic penal and commercial law. But even president Zia kept Islam at bay in political and economic matters, where his policy was avowedly secularist. Since his death in a plane crash in 1988, Pakistani politics has been dominated by ethnic tension, rivalries, and corruption scandals among members of the elite classes, and the Islamists have been less influential. Islam remains important to Pakistan's identity and is ubiquitous in public life, but it still does not affect realpolitik. The compromise is reminiscent of the solutions of the Abbasids and Mongols, which saw a similar separation of powers. The state seems to have forced the Islamic parties into line, but this state of affairs is far from ideal. As in India, disproportionate sums are spent on nuclear weapons, while at least a third of the population languishes in hopeless poverty, a situation which is abhorrent to a truly Muslim sensibility. Muslim activists who feel coerced by the state look toward the fundamentalist government of the Taliban in neighboring Afghanistan.

The fact that Muslims have not yet found an ideal polity for the twentieth century does not mean that Islam is incompatible with modernity. The struggle to enshrine the Islamic ideal in state structures and to find the right leader has preoccupied Muslims throughout their history. Because, like any religious value, the notion of the true Islamic state is transcendent, it can never be perfectly expressed in human form and always eludes the grasp of frail and flawed human beings. Religious life is difficult, and the secular rationalism of our modern culture poses special problems for people in all the major traditions. Christians, who are more preoccupied by doctrine than by politics, are currently wrestling with dogmatic questions in their effort to make their faith speak to the modern sensibility. They are debating their belief in the divinity of Christ, for example, some clinging to the older formulations of the dogma, others finding more radical solutions. Sometimes these discussions become anguished and even acrimonious, because the issues touch the nub of religiosity that lies at the heart of the Christian vision. The struggle for a modern Islamic state is the Muslim equivalent of this dilemma. All religious people in any age have to make their traditions address the challenge of their particular modernity, and the quest for an ideal form of Muslim government should not be viewed as aberrant but as an essentially and typically religious activity.

The Western media often give the impression that the embattled and occasionally violent form of religiosity know as "fundamentalism" is a purely Islamic phenomenon. This is not the case. Fundamentalism is a global fact and has surfaced in every major faith in response to the problems of our modernity. There is fundamentalist Judaism, fundamentalist Christianity, fundamentalist Hinduism, fundamentalist Buddhism, fundamentalist Sikhism, and even fundamentalist Confucianism. This type of faith surfaced first in the Christian world in the United States at the beginning of the twentieth century. This was not accidental. Fundamentalism is not a monolithic movement; each form of fundamentalism, even within the same tradition, develops independently and has its own symbols and enthusiasms, but its different manifestations all bear a family resemblance. It has been noted that a fundamentalist movement does not arise immediately, as a knee-jerk response to the advent of Western modernity, but only takes shape when the modernization process is quite far advanced. At first religious people try to reform their traditions and effect a marriage between them and modern culture, as we have seen the Muslim reformers do. But when these moderate measures are found to be of no avail, some people resort to more extreme methods, and a fundamentalist movement is born. With hindsight, we can see that it was only to be expected that fundamentalism should first make itself known in the United States, the showcase of modernity, and only appear in other parts of the world at a later date. Of the three monotheistic religions, Islam was in fact the last to develop a fundamentalist strain, when modern culture began to take root in the Muslim world in the late 1960s and 1970s. By this date, fundamentalism was quite well established among Christians and Jews, who had had a longer exposure to the modern experience.

Fundamentalist movements in all faiths share certain characteristics. They reveal a deep disappointment and disenchantment with the modern experiment, which has not fulfilled all that it promised. They also express real fear. Every single fundamentalist movement that I have studied is convinced that the secular establishment is determined to wipe religion out. This is not always a paranoid reaction. We have seen that secularism has often been imposed very aggressively in the Muslim world. Fundamentalists look back to a "golden age" before the irruption of modernity for inspiration, but they are not atavistically returning to the Middle Ages. All are intrinsically modern movements and could have appeared at no time other than our own. All are innovative and often radical in their reinterpretation of religion. As such, fundamentalism is an essential part of the modern scene. Wherever modernity takes root, a fundamentalist movement is likely to rise up alongside it in conscious reaction. Fundamentalists will often express their discontent with a modern development by overstressing those elements in their tradition that militate against it. They are all — even in the United States — highly critical of democracy and secularism. Because the emancipation of women has been one of the hallmarks of modern culture, fundamentalists tend to emphasize conventional, agrarian gender roles, putting women back into veils and into the home. The fundamentalist community can thus be seen as the shadow-side of modernity; it can also highlight some of the darker sides of the modern experiment.

Fundamentalism, therefore, exists in a symbiotic relationship with a coercive secularism. Fundamentalists nearly always feel assaulted by the liberal or modernizing establishment, and their views and behavior become more extreme as a result. After the famous Scopes Trial (1925) in Tennessee, when Protestant fundamentalists tried to prevent the teaching of evolution in the public schools, they were so ridiculed by the secularist press that their theology became more reactionary and excessively literal, and they turned from the left to the extreme right of the political spectrum. When the secularist attack has been more violent, the fundamentalist reaction is likely to be even greater. Fundamentalism therefore reveals a fissure in society, which is polarized between those who enjoy secular culture and those who regard it with dread. As time passes, the two camps become increasingly unable to understand one another. Fundamentalism thus begins as an internal dispute, with liberalizers or secularists within one's own culture or nation. In the first instance, for example, Muslim fundamentalists will often oppose their fellow countrymen or fellow Muslims who take a more positive view of modernity, rather than such external foes as the West or Israel. Very often, fundamentalists begin by withdrawing from mainstream culture to create an enclave of pure faith (as, for example, within the ultra-Orthodox Jewish communities in Jerusalem or New York). Thence they will sometimes conduct an offensive which can take many forms, designed to bring the mainstream back to the right path and resacralize the world. All fundamentalists feel that they are fighting for survival, and because their backs are to the wall, they can believe that they have to fight their way out of the impasse. In this frame of mind, on rare occasions, some resort to terrorism. The vast majority, however, do not commit acts of violence, but simply try to revive their faith in a more conventional, lawful way.

Fundamentalists have been successful in so far as they have pushed religion from the sidelines and back to center stage, so that it now plays a major part in international affairs once again, a development that would have seemed inconceivable in the mid-twentieth century when secularism seemed in the ascendant. This has certainly been the case in the Islamic world since the 1970s. But fundamentalism is not simply a way of "using" religion for political end. These are essentially rebellions against the secularist exclusion of the divine from public life, and a frequently desperate attempt to make spiritual values prevail in the modern world. But the desperation and fear that fuel fundamentalists also tend to distort the religious tradition, and accentuate its more aggressive aspects at the expense of those that preach toleration and reconciliation.

Muslim fundamentalism corresponds very closely to these general characteristics. It is not correct, therefore, to imagine that Islam has within it a militant, fanatic strain that impels Muslims into a crazed and violent rejection of modernity. Muslims are in tune with fundamentalists in other faiths all over the world, who share their profound misgivings about modern secular culture. It should also be said that Muslims object to the use of the term "fundamentalism," pointing out quite correctly that it was coined by American Protestants as a badge of pride, and cannot be usefully translated into Arabic. Usul refers to the fundamental principles of Islamic jurisprudence, and as all Muslims agree on these, all Muslims could be said to subscribe to *usuliyyah* (fundamentalism). Nevertheless, for all its shortcomings, "fundamentalism" is the only term we have to describe this family of embattled religious movements, and it is difficult to come up with a more satisfactory substitute. . . .

On the eve of the second Christian millennium, the Crusaders massacred some thirty thousand Jews and Muslims in Jerusalem, turning the thriving Islamic holy city into a stinking charnel house. For at least five months the valleys and ditches around the city were filled with putrefying corpses, which were too numerous for the small number of Crusaders who remained behind after the expedition to clear away, and a stench hung over Jerusalem, where the three religions of Abraham had been able to coexist in relative harmony under Islamic rule for nearly five hundred years. This was the Muslims' first experience of the Christian West, as it pulled itself out of the dark age that had descended after the collapse of the Roman Empire in the fifth century, and fought its way back on to the international scene. The Muslims suffered from the Crusaders, but were not long incommoded by their presence. In 1187 Saladin was able to recapture Jerusalem for Islam and though the Crusaders hung on in the Near East for another century, they seemed an unimportant passing episode in the long Islamic history of the region. Most of the inhabitants of Islamdon were entirely unaffected by the Crusades and remained uninterested in western Europe, which, despite its dramatic cultural advance during the crusading period, still lagged behind the Muslim world.

Europeans did not forget the Crusades, however, nor could they ignore the Dar al-Islam, which, as the years went by, seemed to rule the entire globe. Ever since the Crusades, the people of Western Christendom developed a stereotypical and distorted image of Islam, which they regarded as the enemy of decent civilization. The prejudice became entwined with European fantasies about Jews, the other victims of the Crusaders, and often reflected buried worry about the conduct of Christians. It was, for example, during the Crusades, when it was Christians who had instigated a series of brutal holy wars against the Muslim world, that Islam was described by the learned scholar-monks of Europe as an inherently violent and intolerant faith, which had only been able to establish itself by the sword. The myth of the supposed fanatical intolerance of Islam has become one of the received ideas of the West.

As the millennium drew to a close, however, some Muslims seemed to live up to this Western perception, and, for the first time, have made sacred violence a cardinal Islamic duty. These fundamentalists often call Western colonialism and post-colonial Western imperialism *al-Salibiyyah*: the Crusade. The colonial crusade has been less violent but its impact has been more devastating than the medieval holy wars. The powerful Muslim world has been reduced to a dependent bloc, and Muslim society has been gravely dislocated in the course of an accelerated modernization programme. All over the world, as we have seen, people in all the major faiths have reeled under the impact of Western modernity, and have produced the embattled and frequently intolerant religiosity that they call fundamentalism. As they struggle to rectify what they see as the damaging effects of modern secular culture, fundamentalists fight back and, in the process, they depart from the core values of compassion, justice, and benevolence that characterize all the world faiths, including Islam. Religion, like any other human activity, is often abused, but at its best it helps human beings to cultivate a sense of the sacred inviolability of each individual, and thus to mitigate the murderous violence to which our species is tragically prone. Religion has committed atrocities in the past, but in its brief history secularism has proved that it can be just as violent. As we have seen, secular aggression and persecution have often led to a heightening of religious intolerance and hatred. . . .

It is not true that Muslims are now uniformly filled with hatred of the West. In the early stages of modernization, many leading thinkers were infatuated with European culture, and by the end of the twentieth century some of the most eminent and influential Muslim thinkers were now reaching out to the West again. President Khatami of Iran is only one example of this trend. So is the Iranian intellectual Abdolkarim Sorush, who held important posts in Khomeini's government, and though he is often harried by the more conservative *mujtahids*, he strongly influences those in power. Sorush admires Khomeini, but has moved beyond him. He maintains that Iranians now have three identities: pre-Islamic, Islamic, and Western, which they must try to reconcile. Sorush rejects the secularism of the West and believes that human beings will always need spirituality, but advises Iranians to study the modern sciences, while holding on to Shii tradition. Islam must develop its *fiqh*, so as to accommodate the modern industrial world, and evolve a philosophy of civil rights and an economic theory capable of holding its own in the twenty-first century.

Sunni thinkers have come to similar conclusions. Western hostility toward Islam springs from ignorance, Rashid al-Ghannouchi, the leader of the exiled Renaissance Party in Tunisia, believes. It also springs from a bad experience of Christianity, which did stifle thought and creativity. He describes himself as a "democratic Islamist" and sees no incompatibility between Islam and democracy, but he rejects the secularism of the West, because the human being cannot be so divided and fragmented. The Muslim ideal of *tawhid* rejects the duality of body and spirit, intellect and spirituality, men and women, morality and the economy, East and West. Muslims want modernity, but not one that has been imposed upon them by America,

Britain, or France. Muslims admire the efficiency and beautiful technology of the West; they are fascinated by the way a regime can be changed in the West without bloodshed. But when Muslims look at Western society, they see no light, no heart and no spirituality. They want to hold on to their own religious and moral traditions and, at the same time, to try to incorporate some of the best aspects of Western civilization. Yusuf Abdallah al-Qaradawi, a graduate of al-Azhar, and a Muslim Brother, who is currently the director of the Centre for Sunnah and Sirah at the University of Qatar, takes a similar line. He believes in moderation, and is convinced that the bigotry that has recently appeared in the Muslim world will impoverish people be depriving them of the insights and visions of other human beings. The Prophet Muhammad said that he had come to bring a "Middle Way" of religious life that shunned extremes, and Qaradawi thinks that the current extremism in some quarters of the Islamic world is alien to the Muslim spirit and will not last. Islam is a religion of peace, as the Prophet had shown when he made an unpopular treaty with the Quraysh at Hudaybiyyah, a feat which the Qur'an calls "a great victory." The West, he insists, must learn to recognize the Muslims' right to live their religion and, if they choose, to incorporate the Islamic ideal in their polity. They have to appreciate that there is more than one way of life. Variety benefits the whole world. God gave human beings the right and ability to choose, and some may opt for a religious way of life — including an Islamic state — while others prefer the secular ideal.

"It is better for the West that Muslims should be religious," Qaradawi argues, "hold to their religion, and try to be moral." He raises an important point. Many Western people are also becoming uncomfortable about the absence of spirituality in their lives. They do not necessarily want to return to pre-modern religious lifestyles or to conventionally institutional faith. But there is a growing appreciation that, at its best, religion has helped human beings to cultivate decent values. Islam kept the notions of social justice, equality, tolerance, and practical compassion in the forefront of the Muslim conscience for centuries. Muslims did not always live up to these ideals and frequently found difficulty in incarnating them in their social and political institutions. But the struggle to achieve this was for centuries the mainspring of Islamic spirituality. Western people must become aware that it is in their interests too that Islam remains healthy and strong. The West has not been wholly responsible for the extreme forms of Islam, which have cultivated a violence that violates the most sacred canons of religion. But the West has certainly contributed to this development and, to assuage the fear and despair that lie at the root of all fundamentalist vision, should cultivate a more accurate appreciation of Islam in the third Christian millennium.

BERNARD LEWIS

The Roots of Muslim Rage

I SLAM IS ONE of the world's great religions. Let me be explicit about what I, as a historian of Islam who is not a Muslim, mean by that. Islam has brought comfort and peace of mind to countless millions of men and women. It has given dignity and meaning to drab and impoverished lives. It has taught people of different races to live in brotherhood and people of different creeds to live side by side in reasonable tolerance. It inspired a great civilization in which others besides Muslims lived creative and useful lives and which, by its achievement, enriched the whole world. But Islam, like other religions, has also known periods when it inspired in some of its followers a mood of hatred and violence. It is our misfortune that part, though by no means all or

BERNARD LEWIS *is Professor Emeritus at Princeton University. He has studied Middle Eastern history for more than 60 years and is the author of numerous books on Islam, including the best-selling* Islam and the West. *His seminal piece "The Roots of Muslim Rage" originally appeared in the* Atlantic Monthly *in 1990.*

even most, of the Muslim world is now going through such a period, and that much, though again not all, of that hatred is directed against us. . . .

At times this hatred goes beyond hostility to specific interests or actions or policies or even countries and becomes a rejection of Western civilization as such, not only what it does but what it is, and the principles and values that it practices and professes. These are indeed seen as innately evil, and those who promote or accept them as the "enemies of God."

This phrase, which recurs so frequently in the language of the Iranian leadership, in both their judicial proceedings and their political pronouncements, must seem very strange to the modern outsider, whether religious or secular. The idea that God has enemies, and needs human help in order to identify and dispose of them, is a little difficult to assimilate. It is not, however, all that alien. The concept of the enemies of God is familiar in preclassical and classical antiquity, and in both the Old and New Testaments, as well as in the Qur'an. A particularly relevant version of the idea occurs in the dualist religions of ancient Iran, whose cosmogony assumed not one but two supreme powers. The Zoroastrian devil, unlike the Christian or Muslim or Jewish devil, is not one of God's creatures performing some of God's more mysterious tasks but an independent power, a supreme force of evil engaged in a cosmic struggle against God. This belief influenced a number of Christian, Muslim, and Jewish sects, through Manichaeism and other routes. The almost forgotten religion of the Manichees has given its name to the perception of problems as a stark and simple conflict between matching forces of pure good and pure evil.

The Qur'an is of course strictly monotheistic, and recognizes one God, one universal power only. There is a struggle in human hearts between good and evil, between God's commandments and the tempter, but this is seen as a struggle ordained by God, with its outcome preordained by God, serving as a test of mankind, and not, as in some of the old dualist religions, a struggle in which mankind has a crucial part to play in bringing about the victory of good over evil. Despite this monotheism, Islam, like Judaism and Christianity, was at various stages influenced, especially in Iran, by the dualist idea of a cosmic clash of good and evil, light and darkness, order and chaos, truth and falsehood, God and the Adversary, variously known as devil, Iblis, Satan, and by other names.

The Rise of the House of Unbelief

IN ISLAM THE STRUGGLE of good and evil very soon acquired political and even military dimensions. Muhammad, it will be recalled, was not only a prophet and a teacher, like the founders of other religions; he was also the head of a polity and of a community, a ruler and a soldier. Hence his struggle involved a state and its armed forces. If the fighters in the war for Islam, the holy war "in the path of God," are fighting for God, it follows that their opponents are fighting against God. And since God is in principle the sovereign, the supreme head of the Islamic state — and the Prophet and, after the Prophet, the caliphs are his vicegerents — then God as sovereign commands the army. The army is God's army and the enemy is God's enemy. The duty of God's soldiers is to dispatch God's enemies as quickly as possible to the place where God will chastise them — that is to say, the afterlife.

Clearly related to this is the basic division of mankind as perceived in Islam. Most, probably all, human societies have a way of distinguishing between themselves and others: insider and outsider, in-group and out-group, kinsman or neighbor and foreigner. These definitions not only define the outsider but also, and perhaps more particularly, help to define and illustrate our perception of ourselves.

In the classical Islamic view, to which many Muslims are beginning to return, the world and all mankind are divided into two: the House of Islam, where the Muslim law and faith prevail, and the rest, known as the House of Unbelief or the House of War, which it is the duty of Muslims ultimately to bring to Islam. But the greater part of the world is still outside Islam, and even inside the Islamic lands, according to the view of the Muslim radicals, the faith of Islam has been undermined and the law of Islam has been abrogated. The obligation of holy war therefore begins at home and continues abroad, against the same infidel enemy.

Like every other civilization known to human history, the Muslim world in its heyday saw itself as the center of truth and enlightenment, surrounded by infidel barbarians whom it would in due course enlighten and civilize. But between the different groups of barbarians there was a crucial difference. The barbarians to the east and the south were polytheists and idolaters, offering no serious threat and no competition at all to Islam. In the north and west, in contrast, Muslims from an early date recognized a genuine rival — a competing world religion, a distinctive civilization inspired by that religion, and an empire that, though much smaller than theirs, was no less ambitious in its claims and aspirations. This was the entity known to itself and others as Christendom, a term that was long almost identical with Europe.

The struggle between these rival systems has now lasted for some fourteen centuries. It began with the advent of Islam, in the seventh century, and has continued virtually to the present day. It has consisted of a long series of attacks and counterattacks, jihads and crusades, conquests and reconquests. For the first thousand years Islam was advancing, Christendom in retreat and under threat. The new faith conquered the old Christian lands of the Levant and North Africa, and invaded Europe, ruling for a while in Sicily, Spain, Portugal, and even parts of France. The attempt by the Crusaders to recover the lost lands of Christendom in the east was held and thrown back, and even the Muslims' loss of southwestern Europe to the Reconquista was amply compensated by the Islamic advance into southeastern Europe, which twice reached as far as Vienna. For the past three hundred years, since the failure of the second Turkish siege of Vienna in 1683 and the rise of the European colonial empires in Asia and Africa, Islam has been on the defensive, and the Christian and post-Christian civilization of Europe and her daughters has brought the whole world, including Islam, within its orbit.

For a long time now there has been a rising tide of rebellion against this Western paramountcy, and a desire to reassert Muslim values and restore Muslim greatness. The Muslim has suffered successive stages of defeat. The first was his loss of domination in the world, to the advancing power of Russia and the West. The second was the undermining of his authority in his own country, through an invasion of foreign ideas and laws and ways of life and sometimes even foreign rulers or settlers, and the enfranchisement of native non-Muslim elements. The third — the last straw — was the challenge to his mastery in his own house, from emancipated women and rebellious children. It was too much to endure, and the outbreak of rage against these alien, infidel, and incomprehensible forces that had subverted his dominance, disrupted his society, and finally violated the sanctuary of his home was inevitable. It was also natural that this rage should be directed primarily against the millennial enemy and should draw its strength from ancient beliefs and loyalties.

Europe and her daughters? The phrase may seem odd to Americans, whose national myths, since the beginning of their nationhood and even earlier, have usually defined their very identity in opposition to Europe, as something new and radically different from the old European ways. This is not, however, the way that others have seen it; not often in Europe, and hardly ever elsewhere.

Though people of other races and cultures participated, for the most part involuntarily, in the discovery and creation of the Americas, this was, and in the eyes of the rest of the world long remained, a European enterprise, in which Europeans predominated and dominated and to which

Europeans gave their languages, their religions, and much of their way of life.

For a very long time voluntary immigration to America was almost exclusively European. There were indeed some who came from the Muslim lands in the Middle East and North Africa, but few were Muslims; most were members of the Christian and to a lesser extent the Jewish minorities in those countries. Their departure for America, and their subsequent presence in America, must have strengthened rather than lessened the European image of America in Muslim eyes.

In the lands of Islam remarkably little was known about America. At first the voyages of discovery aroused some interest; the only surviving copy of Columbus's own map of America is a Turkish translation and adaptation, still preserved in the Topkapi Palace Museum, in Istanbul. A sixteenth-century Turkish geographer's account of the discovery of the New World, titled *The History of Western India*, was one of the first books printed in Turkey. But thereafter interest seems to have waned, and not much is said about America in Turkish, Arabic, or other Muslim languages until a relatively late date. A Moroccan ambassador who was in Spain at the time wrote what must surely be the first Arabic account of the American Revolution. The Sultan of Morocco signed a treaty of peace and friendship with the United States in 1787, and thereafter the new republic had a number of dealings, some friendly, some hostile, most commercial, with other Muslim states. These seem to have had little impact on either side. The American Revolution and the American republic to which it gave birth long remained unnoticed and unknown. Even the small but growing American presence in Muslim lands in the nineteenth century — merchants, consuls, missionaries, and teachers — aroused little or no curiosity, and is almost unmentioned in the Muslim literature and newspapers of the time.

The Second World War, the oil industry, and postwar developments brought many Americans to the Islamic lands; increasing numbers of Muslims also came to America, first as students, then as teachers or businessmen or other visitors, and eventually as immigrants. Cinema and later television brought the American way of life, or at any rate a certain version of it, before countless millions to whom the very name of America had previously been meaningless or unknown. A wide range of American products, particularly in the immediate postwar years, when European competition was virtually eliminated and Japanese competition had not yet arisen, reached into the remotest markets of the Muslim world, winning new customers and, perhaps more important, creating new tastes and ambitions. For some, America represented freedom and justice and opportunity. For many more, it represented wealth and power and success, at a time when these qualities were not regarded as sins or crimes.

And then came the great change, when the leaders of a widespread and widening religious revival sought out and identified their enemies as the enemies of God, and gave them "a local habitation and a name" in the Western Hemisphere. Suddenly, or so it seemed, America had become the archenemy, the incarnation of evil, the diabolic opponent of all that is good, and specifically, for Muslims, of Islam. Why? . . .

Some Familiar Accusations

THE ACCUSATIONS are familiar. We of the West are accused of sexism, racism, and imperialism, institutionalized in patriarchy and slavery, tyranny and exploitation. To these charges, and to others as heinous, we have no option but to plead guilty — not as Americans, nor yet as Westerners, but simply as human beings, as members of the human race. In none of these sins are we the only sinners, and in some of them we are very far from being the worst. The treatment of women in the Western world, and more generally in Christendom, has always been unequal and often oppressive, but even at its worst it was rather better than the rule of polygamy and concubinage that has otherwise been the almost universal lot of womankind on this planet.

Is racism, then, the main grievance? Certainly the word figures prominently in publicity addressed to Western, Eastern European, and some Third World audiences. It figures less prominently in what is written and published for home consumption, and has become a generalized and meaningless term of abuse — rather like "fascism," which is nowadays imputed to opponents even by spokesmen for one-party, nationalist dictatorships of various complexions and shirt colors.

Slavery is today universally denounced as an offense against humanity, but within living memory it has been practiced and even defended as a necessary institution, established and regulated by divine law. The peculiarity of the peculiar institution, as Americans once called it, lay not in its existence but in its abolition. Westerners were the first to break the consensus of acceptance and to outlaw slavery, first at home, then in the other territories they controlled, and finally wherever in the world they were able to exercise power or influence — in a word, by means of imperialism.

Is imperialism, then, the grievance? Some Western powers, and in a sense Western civilization as a whole, have certainly been guilty of imperialism, but are we really to believe that in the expansion of Western Europe there was a quality of moral delinquency lacking in such earlier, relatively innocent expansions as those of the Arabs or the Mongols or the Ottomans, or in more recent expansions such as that which brought the rulers of Muscovy to the Baltic, the Black Sea, the Caspian, the Hindu Kush, and the Pacific Ocean? In having practiced sexism, racism, and imperialism, the West was merely following the common practice of mankind through the millennia of recorded history. Where it is distinct from all other civilizations is in having recognized, named, and tried, not entirely without success, to remedy these historic diseases. And that is surely a matter for congratulation, not condemnation. We do not hold Western medical science in general, or Dr. Parkinson and Dr. Alzheimer in particular, responsible for the diseases they diagnosed and to which they gave their names.

Of all these offenses the one that is most widely, frequently, and vehemently denounced is undoubtedly imperialism — sometimes just Western, sometimes Eastern (that is, Soviet) and Western alike. But the way this term is used in the literature of Islamic fundamentalists often suggests that it may not carry quite the same meaning for them as for its Western critics. In many of these writings the term "imperialist" is given a distinctly religious significance, being used in association, and sometimes interchangeably, with "missionary," and denoting a form of attack that includes the Crusades as well as the modern colonial empires. One also sometimes gets the impression that the offense of imperialism is not — as for Western critics — the domination by one people over another but rather the allocation of roles in this relationship. What is truly evil and unacceptable is the domination of infidels over true believers. For true believers to rule misbelievers is proper and natural, since this provides for the maintenance of the holy law, and gives the misbelievers both the opportunity and the incentive to embrace the true faith. But for misbelievers to rule over true believers is blasphemous and unnatural, since it leads to the corruption of religion and morality in society, and to the flouting or even the abrogation of God's law. This may help us to understand the current troubles in such diverse places as Ethiopian Eritrea, Indian Kashmir, Chinese Sinkiang, and Yugoslav Kossovo, in all of which Muslim populations are ruled by non-Muslim governments. It may also explain why spokesmen for the new Muslim minorities in Western Europe demand for Islam a degree of legal protection which those countries no longer give to Christianity and have never given to Judaism. Nor, of course, did the governments of the countries of origin of these Muslim spokesmen ever accord such protection to religions other than their own. In their perception, there is no contradiction in these attitudes. The true faith, based on God's final revelation, must be protected from insult and abuse; other faiths, being either false or incomplete, have no right to any such protection.

There are other difficulties in the way of accepting imperialism as an explanation of Muslim hostility, even if we define imperialism narrowly and specifically, as the invasion and domination of Muslim countries by non-Muslims. If the hostility is directed against imperialism in that sense, why has it been so much stronger against Western Europe, which has relinquished all its Muslim possessions and dependencies, than against Russia, which still rules, with no light hand, over many millions of reluctant Muslim subjects and over ancient Muslim cities and countries? And why should it include the United States, which, apart from a brief interlude in the Muslim-minority area of the Philippines, has never ruled any Muslim population? The last surviving European empire with Muslim subjects, that of the Soviet Union, far from being the target of criticism and attack, has been almost exempt. Even the most recent repressions of Muslim revolts in the southern and central Asian republics of the USSR incurred no more than relatively mild words of expostulation, coupled with a disclaimer of any desire to interfere in what are quaintly called the "internal affairs" of the USSR and a request for the preservation of order and tranquillity on the frontier.

One reason for this somewhat surprising restraint is to be found in the nature of events in Soviet Azerbaijan. Islam is obviously an important and potentially a growing element in the Azerbaijani sense of identity, but it is not at present a dominant element, and the Azerbaijani movement has more in common with the liberal patriotism of Europe than with Islamic fundamentalism. Such a movement would not arouse the sympathy of the rulers of the Islamic Republic. It might even alarm them, since a genuinely democratic national state run by the people of Soviet Azerbaijan would exercise a powerful attraction on their kinsmen immediately to the south, in Iranian Azerbaijan.

Another reason for this relative lack of concern for the 50 million or more Muslims under Soviet rule may be a calculation of risk and advantage. The Soviet Union is near, along the northern frontiers of Turkey, Iran, and Afghanistan; America and even Western Europe are far away. More to the point, it has not hitherto been the practice of the Soviets to quell disturbances with water cannon and rubber bullets, with TV cameras in attendance, or to release arrested persons on bail and allow them access to domestic and foreign media. The Soviets do not interview their harshest critics on prime time, or tempt them with teaching, lecturing, and writing engagements. On the contrary, their ways of indicating displeasure with criticism can often be quite disagreeable.

But fear of reprisals, though no doubt important, is not the only or perhaps even the principal reason for the relatively minor place assigned to the Soviet Union, as compared with the West, in the demonology of fundamentalism. After all, the great social and intellectual and economic changes that have transformed most of the Islamic world, and given rise to such commonly denounced Western evils as consumerism and secularism, emerged from the West, not from the Soviet Union. No one could accuse the Soviets of consumerism;

their materialism is philosophic — to be precise, dialectical — and has little or nothing to do in practice with providing the good things of life. Such provision represents another kind of materialism, often designated by its opponents as crass. It is associated with the capitalist West and not with the communist East, which has practiced, or at least imposed on its subjects, a degree of austerity that would impress a Sufi saint.

Nor were the Soviets, until very recently, vulnerable to charges of secularism, the other great fundamentalist accusation against the West. Though atheist, they were not godless, and had in fact created an elaborate state apparatus to impose the worship of their gods — an apparatus with its own orthodoxy, a hierarchy to define and enforce it, and an armed inquisition to detect and extirpate heresy. The separation of religion from the state does not mean the establishment of irreligion by the state, still less the forcible imposition of an anti-religious philosophy. Soviet secularism, like Soviet consumerism, holds no temptation for the Muslim masses, and is losing what appeal it had for Muslim intellectuals. More than ever before it is Western capitalism and democracy that provide an authentic and attractive alternative to traditional ways of thought and life. Fundamentalist leaders are not mistaken in seeing in Western civilization the greatest challenge to the way of life that they wish to retain or restore for their people.

A Clash of Civilizations

THE ORIGINS OF secularism in the West may be found

in two circumstances — in early Christian teachings and, still more, experience, which created two institutions, Church and State; and in later Christian conflicts, which drove the two apart. Muslims, too, had their religious disagreements, but there was nothing remotely approaching the ferocity of the Christian struggles between Protestants and Catholics, which devastated Christian Europe in the sixteenth and seventeenth centuries and finally drove Christians in desperation to evolve a doctrine of the separation of religion from the state. Only by depriving religious institutions of coercive power, it seemed, could Christendom restrain the murderous intolerance and persecution that Christians had visited on followers of other religions and, most of all, on those who professed other forms of their own.

Muslims experienced no such need and evolved no such doctrine. There was no need for secularism in Islam, and even its pluralism was very different from that of the pagan Roman Empire, so vividly described by Edward Gibbon when he remarked that "the various modes of worship, which prevailed in the Roman world, were all considered by the people, as equally true; by the philosopher, as equally false; and by the magistrate, as equally useful." Islam was never prepared, either in theory or in practice, to accord full equality to those who held other beliefs and practiced other forms of worship. It did, however, accord to the holders of partial truth a degree of practical as well as theoretical tolerance rarely paralleled in the Christian world until the West adopted a measure of secularism in the late-seventeenth and eighteenth centuries.

At first the Muslim response to Western civilization was

one of admiration and emulation — an immense respect for the achievements of the West, and a desire to imitate and adopt them. This desire arose from a keen and growing awareness of the weakness, poverty, and backwardness of the Islamic world as compared with the advancing West. The disparity first became apparent on the battlefield but soon spread to other areas of human activity. Muslim writers observed and described the wealth and power of the West, its science and technology, its manufactures, and its forms of government. For a time the secret of Western success was seen to lie in two achievements: economic advancement and especially industry; political institutions and especially freedom. Several generations of reformers and modernizers tried to adapt these and introduce them to their own countries, in the hope that they would thereby be able to achieve equality with the West and perhaps restore their lost superiority.

In our own time this mood of admiration and emulation has, among many Muslims, given way to one of hostility and rejection. In part this mood is surely due to a feeling of humiliation — a growing awareness, among the heirs of an old, proud, and long dominant civilization, of having been overtaken, overborne, and overwhelmed by those whom they regarded as their inferiors. In part this mood is due to events in the Western world itself. One factor of major importance was certainly the impact of two great suicidal wars, in which Western civilization tore itself apart, bringing untold destruction to its own and other peoples, and in which the belligerents conducted an immense propaganda effort, in the Islamic world and elsewhere, to discredit and undermine each other. The message they brought found many listeners, who were all the more ready to respond in that their own experience of Western ways was not happy. The introduction of Western commercial, financial, and industrial methods did indeed bring great wealth, but it accrued to transplanted Westerners and members of Westernized minorities, and to only a few among the mainstream Muslim population. In time these few became more numerous, but they remained isolated from the masses, differing from them even in their dress and style of life. Inevitably they were seen as agents of and collaborators with what was once again regarded as a hostile world. Even the political institutions that had come from the West were discredited, being judged not by their Western originals but by their local imitations, installed by enthusiastic Muslim reformers. These, operating in a situation beyond their control, using imported and inappropriate methods that they did not fully understand, were unable to cope with the rapidly developing crises and were one by one overthrown. For vast numbers of Middle Easterners, Western-style economic methods brought poverty, Western-style political institutions brought tyranny, even Western-style warfare brought defeat. It is hardly surprising that so many were willing to listen to voices telling them that the old Islamic ways were best and that their only salvation was to throw aside the pagan innovations of the reformers and return to the True Path that God had prescribed for his people.

Ultimately, the struggle of the fundamentalists is against two enemies, secularism and modernism. The war against secularism is conscious and explicit, and there is by now a whole literature denouncing secularism as an evil neo-pagan force in the modern world and attributing it variously to the Jews, the West, and the United States. The war against modernity is for the most part neither conscious nor explicit, and is directed against the whole process of change that has taken place in the Islamic world in the past century or more and has transformed the political, economic, social, and even cultural structures of Muslim countries. Islamic fundamentalism has given an aim and a form to the otherwise aimless and formless resentment and anger of the Muslim masses at the forces that have devalued their traditional values and loyalties and, in the final analysis, robbed them of their beliefs, their aspirations, their dignity, and to an increasing extent even their livelihood.

There is something in the religious culture of Islam which inspired, in even the humblest peasant or peddler, a dignity and a courtesy toward others never exceeded and rarely equalled in other civilizations. And yet, in moments of upheaval and disruption, when the deeper passions are stirred, this dignity and courtesy toward others can give way to an explosive mixture of rage and hatred which impels even the government of an ancient and civilized country — even the spokesman of a great spiritual and ethical religion — to espouse kidnapping and assassination, and try to find, in the life of their Prophet, approval and indeed precedent for such actions.

The instinct of the masses is not false in locating the ultimate source of these cataclysmic changes in the West and in attributing the disruption of their old way of life to the impact of Western domination, Western influence, or Western precept and example. And since the United States is the legitimate heir of European civilization and the recognized and unchallenged leader of the West, the United States has inherited the resulting grievances and become the focus for the pent-up hate and anger. Two examples may suffice. In November of 1979 an angry mob attacked and burned the U.S. Embassy in Islamabad, Pakistan. The stated cause of the crowd's anger was the seizure of the Great Mosque in Mecca by a group of Muslim dissidents — an event in which there was no American involvement whatsoever. Almost ten years later, in February of 1989, again in Islamabad, the USIS center was attacked by angry crowds, this time to protest the publication of Salman Rushdie's *Satanic Verses*. Rushdie is a British citizen of Indian birth, and his book had been published five months previously in England. But what provoked the mob's anger, and also the Ayatollah Khomeini's subsequent pronouncement of a death sentence on the author, was the publication of the book in the United States.

It should by now be clear that we are facing a mood and a movement far transcending the level of issues and policies and the governments that pursue them. This is no less than a clash of civilizations — the perhaps irrational but surely historic reaction of an ancient rival against our Judeo-Christian heritage, our secular present, and the worldwide expansion of both. It is crucially important that we on our side should not be provoked into an equally historic but also equally irrational reaction against that rival.

Not all the ideas imported from the West by Western

intruders or native Westernizers have been rejected. Some have been accepted by even the most radical Islamic fundamentalists, usually without acknowledgment of source, and suffering a sea change into something rarely rich but often strange. One such was political freedom, with the associated notions and practices of representation, election, and constitutional government. Even the Islamic Republic of Iran has a written constitution and an elected assembly, as well as a kind of episcopate, for none of which is there any prescription in Islamic teaching or any precedent in the Islamic past. All these institutions are clearly adapted from Western models. Muslim states have also retained many of the cultural and social customs of the West and the symbols that express them, such as the form and style of male (and to a much lesser extent female) clothing, notably in the military. The use of Western-invented guns and tanks and planes is a military necessity, but the continued use of fitted tunics and peaked caps is a cultural choice. From constitutions to Coca-Cola, from tanks and television to T-shirts, the symbols and artifacts, and through them the ideas, of the West have retained — even strengthened — their appeal.

The movement nowadays called fundamentalism is not the only Islamic tradition. There are others, more tolerant, more open, that helped to inspire the great achievements of Islamic civilization in the past, and we may hope that these other traditions will in time prevail. But before this issue is decided there will be a hard struggle, in which we of the West can do little or nothing. Even the attempt might do harm, for these are issues that Muslims must decide among themselves. And in the meantime we must take great care on all sides to avoid the danger of a new era of religious wars, arising from the exacerbation of differences and the revival of ancient prejudices.

To this end we must strive to achieve a better appreciation of other religious and political cultures, through the study of their history, their literature, and their achievements. At the same time, we may hope that they will try to achieve a better understanding of ours, and especially that they will understand and respect, even if they do not choose to adopt for themselves, our Western perception of the proper relationship between religion and politics. To describe this perception I shall end with a quotation from an American President, the somewhat unjustly neglected John Tyler, who, in a letter dated July 10, 1843, gave eloquent and indeed prophetic expression to the principle of religious freedom:

> The United States have adventured upon a great and noble experiment, which is believed to have been hazarded in the absence of all previous precedent — that of total separation of Church and State. No religious establishment by law exists among us. The conscience is left free from all restraint and each is permitted to worship his Maker after his own judgement. The offices of the Government are open alike to all. No tithes are levied to support an established Hierarchy, nor is the fallible judgement of man set up as the sure and infallible creed of faith. The Mahommedan, if he will to come among us would

have the privilege guaranteed to him by the constitution to worship according to the Koran; and the East Indian might erect a shrine to Brahma if it so pleased him. Such is the spirit of toleration inculcated by our political Institutions. . . . The Hebrew persecuted and down trodden in other regions takes up his abode among us with none to make him afraid . . . and the Aegis of the Government is over him to defend and protect him. Such is the great experiment which we have tried, and such are the happy fruits which have resulted from it; our system of free government would be imperfect without it.

The body may be oppressed and manacled and yet survive; but if the mind of man be fettered, its energies and faculties perish, and what remains is of the earth, earthly. Mind should be free as the light or as the air.

Women in Islam

I HAVE LEARNED to live by the rhythm of other people's prayers. In Cairo, I woke at sunrise to the voices of *muezzins* and timed my lunch break by the midday call to prayer. There are no *muezzins* where I live now, on a lane of old London houses built two hundred years ago by refugees from France. The refugees, all Catholics, also built a small church by their cottages and so, these days, it is the Angelus bell that wakes me in the morning and sends me to the kitchen at noon in search of food.

One day in the summer of 1992 there was a guest for lunch. A detective arrived first, to search my closets and poke his head into the attic. A filament of dust clung to his hair as he gave the all clear over a walkie-talkie. The cars roared into the lane,

GERALDINE BROOKS's *portrait of the conflicts between Islam and women is from her 1995 book* Nine Parts of Desire. *As a prize-winning foreign corre-spondent for* The Wall Street Journal, *Brooks spent six years covering the Middle East and the daily struggles of Muslim women.*

fast. "Leave the door open now," the detective said. The guest couldn't risk lingering on the doorstep. He entered, suddenly, at the center of a flying wedge of bodyguards. A floppy brown fedora fell low across his face. Sunglasses hid the distinctive droop of his eyelids and the improbable circumflex of his brows. After four years in hiding, Salman Rushdie's skin had the fishlike translucence of a man who never sees the sun. His posture had eased into the self-effacing slouch of an adolescent who desperately doesn't want to be noticed.

I was living in Cairo when the storm broke over *The Satanic Verses*. Just after Khomeini condemned Salman Rushdie to death, I took my copy of the novel to Naguib Mahfouz, Egypt's Nobel laureate, whose own novels had been censored on religious grounds. I hoped he might write a defense of Rushdie: a plea for tolerance, for the freedom of ideas. Mahfouz took the book from my hands and pushed it to the far side of his desk, where he wouldn't have to look at it. He was tired, he said: worn out from his own battles with fundamentalism. He did not think he would enter this engagement.

Perhaps he was wise. On the day Salman Rushdie came to lunch at my house, we talked together for an article I was writing on the chilling effect the fatwa was having on all writers dealing with Islam. I had felt the chill myself, sitting on a sunny terrace in southern Lebanon with a leading cleric of Hezbollah. By then, I was used to the averted gaze of devout Muslim men, and it seemed normal to me to be conversing with someone whose eyes were focused on a floor tile an inch in front of my shoe. He was considering whether to let me meet his wife. He found it troubling that my article would mention the prophet Muhammad's wives and daughters. "You will have to be very careful," he said. Suddenly, he raised his turbaned head and shot me a single, penetrating glare. "Be sure you do not make any mistakes."

Rushdie and I didn't know, as we sat talking of these things, that the Egyptian writer Farag Foda lay dying, that same day, of gunshot wounds inflicted by Islamic jihad in reprisal for his eloquent and often scathing critiques of religious extremism.

In the progressive Shiite magazine *Dialogue*, Ali Allawi writes of the difficulties of potential European converts to Islam in seeing the faith standing separate from "the prejudices and social baggage of Islamic lands." Once Westerners "are able to dissociate Islam from this background noise," he writes, "they are able to quickly appreciate its veracity."

But these days the background noise is very loud. And every day's news seemed to raise the decibels. The World Trade Center explodes on the apparent say-so of a militant Islamic preacher. A United Nations human rights report finds Sudan's Qur'an-based-punishments in conflict with the international human rights agreements the country has signed. In response, the government of Sudan threatens the report's Romanian-born author with death. In Egypt a militant cleric named Ali Yehya commands his followers to tear down the Pyramids and all other pharaonic monuments because civilizations that existed before Islam were base and idolatrous. In Algeria two women are gunned down at a bus stop because they are not veiled. In Saudi Arabia a newspaper editor goes to jail because his English-language newspaper runs a cartoon strip, "BC," that the Saudi government deems heretical. The offending cartoon was a two-frame piece in which a Stone Age man stands on a hill and asks, "God, if you're up there, give me a sign." In the second frame, the man is deluged with a sudden rain shower. "Well," he says, "we know two things: He's up there, and He's got a sense of humor." The Saudis jailed the editor, a Hindu, for running a cartoon strip that questioned the existence of God.

Like the Rushdie fatwa, these incidents come at us from so deep in left field that we, as Westerners, have no coherent way to think about them. We shrug. Weird foreigners. Who understands them? Who needs to?

And yet, as I made my home in London, gradually shaking the last few fine crumbs of Cairo dust from the pages of my books, I found that the background noise of Islam remained always there, in the distance, like a neighbor hammering. And eventually I accepted that it was neither possible nor right to ignore it.

That summer, not long after Salman Rushide came to lunch, I answered the phone to a distraught friend whose neighbor had just been knifed to death. The dead woman was an imam's daughter from the Sudan. She had been stabbed by her husband, also a Sudanese.

It was winter by the time the case came to trial. Every day for five days I walked through a cold London drizzle to a small court in the Old Bailey. To the great machine of British justice, it was a routine case. The press benches were empty.

A simple "domestic" between middle-aged marrieds from a middle-class suburb was too ordinary to be of interest.

The facts of the killing weren't in dispute. Just before dinnertime, in the kitchen of his handsome Victorian house, Omar stabbed his wife, Afaf. With the dripping knife still in his hand, he walked to the phone and called his closest friend to tell him what he had done, and then called the police.

In the small public gallery I sat between the man's brothers and the woman's neighbors. The brothers, who had flown from the Sudan for the trial, shivered in their summerweight suits. The neighbors, well-groomed young mothers who knew the victim from parent-teacher nights and weekday excursions to garden-supply centers, seemed uneasy with the Old Bailey's hard-bitten police procedures. In the gallery they scribbled in notebooks perched on their knees, as if their meticulous records would somehow help them make sense of the thing that had happened on their tranquil, tree-lined street. Just once in the five days, when the barrister for the prosecution held up the weapon — a good-quality Sabatier cook's knife — and questioned a pathologist as to the exact wounds it made when it plunged five times into the victim's chest and abdomen, one of the women put down her pen and sobbed uncontrollably.

At issue in the court was whether the act was a premeditated murder or, as the defense claimed, manslaughter that took place when the accused was temporarily out of his mind as the result of "reaction depression" brought on by the knowledge that his wife had had an affair, and that she had, on the morning of the stabbing, obtained a court order restraining him from taking their children out of Britain to live with his family in the Sudan.

As I listened to the facts of the case, I could interpret them two ways. The Western way, as the jury was interpreting them, led to a description of something we all understood: a crime of passion in a spur-of-the-moment insane frenzy. The other way, the way I'd learned living among the women of Islam, described something very different: a cleansing of family honor, a premeditated killing that would, under British law, draw a sentence of life imprisonment.

From where they sat in their jury box, the men and women of the jury couldn't see Omar as he stood each morning beside his police guard, waiting to be escorted into the court. But from the elevation of the public gallery I could see him, and so could his brothers. Each morning he looked up at them and raised a clenched fist in a defiant victory salute. His step, as he entered the dock, was almost jaunty.

Afaf, thirty-eight years old when she died, was a kinswoman who had been married to him by arrangement. She was barely fifteen; he was already thirty. That Omar was her relative, as well as her husband, mattered perhaps more than any other single fact in the court case. It was as a relation, a male of her blood kin, that tradition deemed him most dishonored by her adultery.

Afaf had made the most of a life that had offered her few choices. She had had no choice when they scraped away her clitoris, married her to a man she barely knew, and sent her thousands of miles from home, to a city whose language she didn't speak.

Afaf lived in London with Omar while he studied for his doctorate. In 1985, unable to find an academic post in Britain, he began work in Saudi Arabia. For ten months of every year Afaf raised her four children alone. While working in clerical jobs, she managed to finish high school and a computer course and to begin a degree in social science. A heavy-set woman with a wide smile and an open manner, she managed to break through British reserve and make friends. For Omar, returning only once a year from Saudi Arabia's austere religious atmosphere, it wasn't so easy. He was hostile to some of Afaf's closest friends, especially an unmarried couple who lived across the street. He felt such neighbors created and "atheistic atmosphere" for his children.

Gradually, the long separations and Afaf's change from docile young wife to an independent, accomplished woman began to fray the marriage's fragile bonds. In 1987, Afaf and Omar stopped sharing a bedroom. Bur Afaf was afraid to ask for a divorce, fearing the Omar would spirit the children back to the Sudan, where Islamic law would give her no right to their custody.

Then one of her work mates, Andrew, a tall, sandy-haired divorce, fell in love with her. At first she kept her distance, but slowly his support at the office extended to help at the house, where the years of Omar's absence had left odd jobs undone and rooms dilapidated. It was Andrew who explained to Afaf that British law would protect her rights to her children. In January 1991 she wrote to her husband asking for a divorcé.

Omar agreed. But then, on his next trip home, he learned

that Andrew had been to his house and even spent the night there once when he'd worked late painting the sunroom. Omar was outraged that the neighbors might have noticed. His main concern was to keep the visits secret, because, he told the court, he was concerned for family honor if Afaf's relationship with another man became public. According to Andrew's testimony at the trial, Omar told him he had no objections to his meeting Afaf, so long as it happened away from her home and the prying gaze of the neighbors.

Afaf may well have lived to divorce Omar and marry the man of her choice if it hadn't been for one long, stressful day of arguments over Omar's right to go out alone with the two younger children, whom Afaf feared he might try to abduct. Omar, frustrated and furious, went to visit his one Sudanese friend, broke down, and confided his suspicions of his wife's infidelity.

That friend, called as a witness in court, described how he'd burst into tears as Omar spoke. Those tears — straight from the heart of a fellow Sudanese who knew the depths of Omar's dishonor — may well have caused Afaf's death. Omar's Western-trained intellect might have been able to win the war with his social baggage if, as he'd intended, his wife's relationship had remained secret. But once his friend knew, the dishonor was an accomplished fact that could be wiped away only in the ancient, bloody way. That Omar's first call after the killing was to this friend — not a doctor, not an ambulance, not the police — seemed to me the strongest evidence of motive presented in the court. Yet the prosecution never made this connection.

At the end of the week the jury reached a manslaughter verdict on the grounds of "diminished responsibility." For ending his wife's life, Omar received a prison sentence of six years. Taking off the time he'd already served since the killing and a likely two-year remission for good behavior, he will probably be free by July 1996.

From the facts presented in that small courtroom, there was little chance of any other verdict. What was missing wasn't evidence but understanding of the prejudices and social baggage of Islamic lands that Omar had carried with him from the Sudan, his country of upbringing, and from Saudi Arabia, the country in which he worked ten months of every year.

Nothing in their own culture or experience equipped this jury of very ordinary-looking English people to comprehend that what had been described in court was an honor killing, one of the hundreds that every year claim Muslim women's lives.

This was not an isolated case; it simply happened to be the one I heard about. In a British study of family violence completed not long after Afaf's death, the researchers found that women married to men of Muslim background were eight times more likely to be killed by their spouses than any other women in Britain. Yet British barristers, judges, and juries continue to assess these crimes by a yardstick that's completely inadequate to measure what is really going on.

Presented with statistics on violence toward women, or facing the furor over the Rushdie fatwa, progressive Muslims such as Ali Allawi, Rana Kabbani, and others ask us to blame a wide range of villains: colonial history, the bitterness of immigrant experience, Bedouin tradition, pre-Islamic African culture. Yet when the Qur'an sanctions wife beating and the execution of apostates, it can't be entirely exonerated for an epidemic of wife slayings and death sentences on authors.

In the end, what Rana Kabbani and Ali Allawi are proposing is as artificial an exercise as that proposed by the Marxists who used to argue that socialism in its pure form should not be maligned and rejected because of the deficiencies of "actually existing socialism." At some point every religion, especially one that purports to encompass a complete way of life and system of government, has to be called to account for the kind of life it offers the people in the lands where it predominates.

It becomes insufficient to look at Islam on paper, or Islam in history, and dwell on the inarguable improvements it brought to women's lives in the seventh century. Today, the much more urgent and relevant task is to examine the way the faith has proved such fertile ground for almost every anti-women custom it encountered in its great march out of Arabia. When it found the veils and seclusion in Persia, it absorbed them; when it found genital mutilations in Egypt, it absorbed them; when it found societies in which women had never had a voice in public affairs, its own traditions of lively women's participation withered.

Yet there are exceptions. When the armies of Islam swept into India, Muslims were appalled by the practice of *sati*, in which widows, on a husbands's death, would burn themselves alive on his funeral pyre. In 1650 the traveler

Jean-Baptiste Tavernier wrote of Hindu widows, banned by their faith from remarriage and reduced by their husband's death to penury and contempt, choosing instead to end their lives through *sati*. "But it should be remarked," he wrote, "that a woman cannot burn herself without having received permission from the governor of the place where she dwells, and those governors who are Musalmans [Muslims] hold this dreadful custom of self-destruction in horror, and do not readily give permission." For those women's saved lives, at least, Islam can take the credit. But why did such a powerful and resilient faith not stand its ground more often in the face of "dreadful customs"?

I have looked everywhere for examples of women trying to reclaim Islam's positive messages, trying to carry forward into the twentieth century the reformist zeal with which Muhammad had remade the lives of many women (other than his own wives and the Muslim army's war captives) in the first Muslim community at Medina. It turned out to be a frustrating search. In most places the direction of the debate seemed to be exactly the reverse. Palestinian, Egyptian, Algerian, and Afghani women were seeing a curtain come down on decades of women's liberation as Islamic leaders in their countries turned to the most exclusionary and inequitable interpretations. For those women who struggled against the tide, the results were a discouraging trio of marginalization, harassment, and exile.

In Morocco, Fatima Mernissi's qur'anic scholarship has made a formidable case for Islam as a religion of equality and human dignity, whose message has simply been buried over time by self-serving misogynists in positions of power. Yet her work is read in Western universities much more than it is in Moroccan mosques. No matter how precise her research into the *hadith*, the male-dominated Islamic establishment doesn't seem willing to open its ears to the scholarship of a Muslim woman who doesn't veil or otherwise flaunt her piety.

Perhaps that is why I found the brightest hope for positive change camouflaged among the black chadors of devout Iranian women. Even the most narrow-minded fundamentalist can't criticize the Islamic credentials of women such as Khomeini's daughter Zahra Mostafavi or Rafsanjani's daughter Faezeh Hashemi. Their conspicuous adherence to religious rules give them a high ground from which to make their case for women's rights. So far, they have used that position sparingly, to get women a greater political voice, more equal job opportunities, and the right to participate in sports. To be sure, these women will never tear down the walls of tradition. They will never make the arguments that can be made within Islamic reasoning against veiling or polygamy. But within those traditional walls they can make a much safer haven for women at risk of abuse and exploitation in the name of Islam.

To Western women, that mightn't look like much. It is easy to see these grim figures in their heavy shrouds as symbols of what's wrong rather than what's right with women and Islam. But to Muslim women elsewhere in the strictest parts of the Islamic world, the Iranian woman riding to work on her motorbike, even with her billowing chador gripped firmly in her teeth, looks like a figure to envy.

"They are our Superwomen," said Iman Fadlallah, the shy twenty-four-year-old wife of the Hezbollah sheik in southern Lebanon who had sat on his terrace and warned me about this article. Iman's father, the most prominent Hezbollah cleric in Beirut, had abruptly ended her schooling when she was fourteen years old, choosing a husband for her whom she didn't meet until the wedding. Now she stayed mainly in her house raising her children. In Iran, where she had lived with her husband while he continued his clerical studies, she had glimpsed a much wider world, even for the most devout of women. She spoke wistfully of Iranian women's opportunities to study and work. "We have to struggle to be as strong as they are," she said.

Everyone has her own way of remembering her travels. Some keep journals. Others take photographs. I go into the bedroom and open my closet. There are memories hanging there semaphores from six years and twenty countries. There is the homespun scarf in red and black, still faintly scented with wood smoke from the cooking fire of the Kurdish woman who untied it from her own hair to wrap around mine. There is the long Palestinian dress Raed's mother Rahme made for me so that I would feel comfortable sitting on the floor among them. I still have the Italian pin-striped "king suit," a discreet little mend hiding the rip from the day I toured with Hussein in the Jordanian desert. I threw out my wedding shoes — the ones with the tide line of camel blood. And I keep meaning to give away the pair of black acrylic socks I had to buy in a hurry when the Islamic dress inspector at a Tehran bank objected to the inch of too-sheer stocking peeking between the top of my shoes and the hem of my chador.

Limp on a hanger is the chador itself, the big black square of silk and synthetic that I used to despise. But that well-worn black rag, stained on the hem and torn on the shoulder, has become an old friend. Like a 1980s dress-for-success suit, it has been the camouflage that helped me do my job in a world where I wasn't quite welcome.

When I look at that chador I no longer get the little shudder of fear or gust of outrage that I used to feel when I saw the most extreme forms of Islamic dress. These days my feelings are much more complex. Chadors are linked in my mind to women I've felt close to, in spite of the abyss of belief that divided us.

When I lived among the women of Islam, I became part of a world that is still, in the last decade of the twentieth century, an intensely private one. In public, most women move like shadows, constrained physically by their hijab or mentally by codes of conduct that inhibit them. It is only behind the high walls and the closed doors that women are ever really free.

For me, entering that world touched emotions that had been a long time dormant. From the time I'd taken my first job, as a cub reporter on the sports desk of *The Sydney Morning Herald*, my career had pushed me into a man's world. When I became a foreign correspondent, most of my colleagues were men. It wasn't until I went to Cairo and started seeking out Muslim women that I realized I hadn't made a close female friend since I left school.

I'd forgotten how much I liked to be with women. And yet there was always a sourness lurking at the edge of even the sweetest encounters. Squatting on the floor of a Kurdish friend's kitchen, helping the women with their bread making, I realized what an agreeable thing it was to be completely surrounded by women, to have a task that was ours alone. As the women's deft fingers flung balls of dough under my rolling pin and the fire roared beneath a baking sheet of blackened metal, I felt contentment in shared work well done.

But an hour into the labor, as my shoulders ached and scalding sweat dribbled down my back, I began to resent the boy toddler who kept ambling up to the steaming pile of fresh bread and breaking off tasty morsels in his fat little fists. His sister, not much older, was already part of our bread-making assembly line. Why should he learn so young that her role was to toil for his pleasure?

The nunlike clothes, pushed to the back of my closet, remind me of all those mixed feeling. Every time my hand brushes the smooth fabric of the chador, I think of Nahid Aghtaie, the Iranian medical student who gave up an easy life in London to go home and work at low-paying jobs to advance the goals of her revolution. I remember her, in Qum, drifting toward me over the marble-floored mosque to tell me that she'd prayed for me "to have nice children." And then I think of her beautiful face — the small visible triangle between brow and lip — radiant on the morning of the murder of Rushdie's Japanese translator in July 1991. "This," she said triumphantly, "shows the power of Islam." I told her that, to me, it no more showed the power of Islam than an Israeli soldier's shooting of a Palestinian child showed the power of Judaism. Why not, I asked her, cite the "power of Islam" in the humanitarian work that Iran was doing for the flood of Iraqi refugees that was then pouring over its borders? "Because nobody notices when we do such things," she said. "But every news report in the world will note this execution."

Eventually I became worn out by such conversations. Friendships with women like Nahid were an emotional whipsaw: How was it possible to admire her for the courage of her convictions, when her convictions led to such hateful reasoning?

Just after that trip to Iran, tired from months of covering the war with Iraq and its aftermath, I went home to Australia for a brief vacation. My plane landed in Sydney just ahead of a flight from Jakarta. As I waited for my luggage, the doors to the arrival hall swished open on a crowd of Indonesian-Australians, waiting to greet their relatives. Almost all of the women were veiled. A swift, mean-spirited thought shot through me jet-lagged brain: "Oh, please. Not here too."

I wasn't raised to be a bigot. My parents considered religious intolerance a sin. My mother had seen too much of it in her childhood, among rural Irish Catholic immigrants. Her mother's marriage to a non-Catholic had been an act of courage. Hers was a typically Australian story: Within two generations she had kicked the dirt of the old country's prejudices from her shoes and adopted Australia's own "religion" — a passionately tolerant secularism. It happened to almost everybody. One of the most revealing statistics I ever learned about my country concerned the twelve members of the Board of Management of Sydney's main synagogue. In 1890 those twelve men were among the city's most observant Jews. Less than a hundred years later, none of the twelve had a single identifiably Jewish descendant. Mixed marriages and the siren song of secularism had claimed them all.

I wondered if that would happen to the new wave of Muslim immigrants. Would their children, too, learn to doubt the Qur'an's doubt-free prescription for how to live? Would they see that Australia, where atheists routinely got elected prime minister, was a much fairer, gentler society than the religious regimes of places like Saudi Arabia and the Sudan? Or would they, as their numbers increased, seek to impose their values on my culture? During the Rushide outcry, Australian Muslims had demonstrated, as was their right. But pictures of their toddlers holding placards saying "Rushdie Must Die" had sent a shudder through the society.

An Iranian-born friend who lives in London, a gentle, middle-aged woman who practices family medicine, says the only war she would willingly fight would be one to stop Islamic fundamentalism telling her how to live her life. She is a Zoroastrian, a member of the ancient Persian faith in which dark and light, good and evil are forever locked in a struggle for supremacy.

Should we also struggle to stop Islamic extremists telling others how to live their lives? As Westerners, we profess to believe that human rights are an immutable international currency, independent of cultural mores and political circumstances. At a Geneva conference on the International

Declaration of Human Rights in 1993, Iran was among a handful of countries that argued otherwise. Cloaking their argument in fashionable dress such as cultural relativism, delegates from Iran and Cuba, China and Indonesia argued that the West had imposed its human rights ideology on nations whose very different religious and political histories gave them the right to choose their own. To me, their argument boiled down to this ghastly and untenable proposition: A human right is what the local despot says it is.

The concept of the universality of human rights prevailed at the conference, and the charter was not amended. And yet the charter has done little so far for the genitally mutilated, the forcibly secluded, the disenfranchised women of the world.

Is it even our fight? As a mental test, I always try to reverse the gender. If some ninety million little boys were having their penises amputated, would the world have acted to prevent it by now? You bet.

Sometimes substituting race for gender also is an interesting exercise. Say a country, a close Western ally and trading partner, had a population half white, half black. The whites had complete control of the blacks. They could beat them if they disobeyed. They deprived them of the right to leave the house without permission; to walk unmolested without wearing the official segregating dress; to hold any decent job in the government, or to work at all without the permission of the white in control of them. Would there have been uproar in our countries by now? Would we have imposed trade sanctions and subjected this country to international opprobrium? You bet. Yet countries such as Saudi Arabia, which deprive half their population of these most basic rights, have been subjected to none of these things.

It is, I suppose, possible to argue that outside pressure is counterproductive when it comes to traditions that are seen to be religious, even if in fact they aren't. Early attempts to ban genital mutilation by colonial-government fiat were dismal failures. But, even if we decline to act on what goes on inside others' borders, there is no excuse for not acting inside our own.

In an era of cultural sensitivity, we need to say that certain cultural baggage is contraband in our countries and will not be admitted. We already draw a line at polygamy; we don't recognize divorce by saying, "I divorce you." We have banned these things even though the Qur'an approves them. It should be easier to take a stand against practices that don't even carry the sanction of the Qur'an. "Honor" killings need to be identified in court and punished as the premeditated murders they are. Young women need to be protected against marriages arranged during hasty "vacations" abroad for teenagers too young to give informed consent. And, most urgent of all, clitoridectomy needs to be made illegal.

In 1994 the United States sill had no laws whatever banning migrants from countries such as Somalia and the Sudan from mutilating the genitals of their daughters, and the operation was taking place in migrant communities throughout the country. The first ever bill on the issue had just been introduced to Congress by Colorado Democrat Patricia Schroeder. While it addressed education of migrants and laws against carrying out mutilations within the United States it didn't propose any means of protecting girls taken out of the country for the procedure.

There is something else we can do: advance the right to asylum on the grounds of "well-founded fear of persecution" to women from any country where fathers, husbands, and brothers claim a religious right to inhibit women's freedom. In January 1993 the Canadian government, after almost two years of consideration, granted asylum to a Saudi student who had requested it on the grounds of gender persecution. It was, they said, "an exception." Why should it be? "Nada," as she asks to be called, experienced the same violent harassment that any woman is subject to from her country's authorities for the "crime" of walking outside her home with uncovered hair. If Nada had remained in Saudi Arabia, and continued to disobey, she might have found herself imprisoned and even tortured, without formal charges ever having been laid.

There is, unfortunately, no chance that granting of automatic asylum to women suffering such gender persecution would lead to a flood of refugees. Only a minority have the means to leave their country, or even their house, when men control the keys to doors and the car and must sign their approval for the shortest of journeys. But such a step would send a signal to regimes whose restrictions have nothing to do with the religion they claim to uphold. And that signal would be that we, too, have certain things we hold sacred: Among them are liberty, equality, the pursuit of happiness and the right to doubt.

It is a long time since I stood under Rafsanjani's gaze at a press conference in Iran and told him I was wearing a chador "in a spirit of mutual respect." At that moment, standing in my black shroud under the hot TV lights, I had a mental image of myself, as I liked to be in summer, bare-skinned on the beach near my parents' home. The "mutual respect" I had in mind demanded that he, and those like him, acknowledge my right to sunbake on those Australian sands and, if I chose, to take *The Satanic Verses* along as my beach reading.

Last year, when I was home in Sydney, I lay on that beach beside a Muslim family who seemed not the least bit troubled by the exposed flesh surrounding them. While the man splashed in the shallows with his toddlers, his wife sat on the sand, her long, loose dress arranged around her. It made me sad that the woman's tiny daughter, splashing so happily with her father and baby brother, would be, one day soon, required to forgo that pleasure. But that would be her fight, not mine. At least, in Australia, she would have a choice. She would choose between her family's values and what she saw elsewhere.

Every now and then the little girl's mother fiddled with her headscarf as it billowed in the sea breeze. That woman had made her choice: It was different from mine. But sitting there, sharing the warm sand and the soft air, we accepted each other. When she raised her face to the sun, she was smiling.

FAREED ZAKARIA

Why They Hate Us

T
O THE QUESTION "Why do the terrorists hate us?" Americans could be pardoned for answering, "Why should we care?" The immediate reaction to the murder of [close to three thousand] innocents is anger, not analysis. Yet anger will not be enough to get us through what is sure to be a long struggle. For that we will need answers.

The ones we have heard so far have been comforting but familiar. We stand for freedom and they hate it. We are rich and they envy us. We are strong and they resent this. All of which is true. But there are billions of poor and weak and oppressed people around the world. They don't turn planes into bombs.

They don't blow themselves up to kill thousands of civilians. If

FAREED ZAKARIA *is the managing editor of* Foreign Affairs *and editor of* Newsweek International. *"Why They Hate Us" is a historical examination of the building tensions between Islam and the West. It originally appeared in* Newsweek *just after the September 11th attacks.*

envy were the cause of terrorism, Beverly Hills, Fifth Avenue, and Mayfair would have become morgues long ago. There is something stronger at work here than deprivation and jealousy. Something that can move men to kill but also to die.

Osama bin Laden has an answer — religion. For him and his followers, this is a holy war between Islam and the Western world. Most Muslims disagree. Every Islamic country in the world has condemned the attacks of September 11. To many, bin Laden belongs to a long line of extremists who have invoked religion to justify mass murder and spur men to suicide. The words "thug," "zealot" and "assassin" all come from ancient terror cults — Hindu, Jewish, and Muslim, respectively — that believed they were doing the work of God. The terrorist's mind is its own place, and like Milton's Satan, can make a hell of heaven, a heaven of hell. Whether it is the Unabomber, Aum Shinrikyo, or Baruch Goldstein (who killed scores of unarmed Muslims in Hebron), terrorists are almost always misfits who place their own twisted morality above mankind's.

But bin Laden and his followers are not an isolated cult like Aum Shinrikyo or the Branch Davidians or demented loners like Timothy McVeigh and the Unabomber. They come out of a culture that reinforces their hostility, distrust, and hatred of the West — and of America in particular. This culture does not condone terrorism but fuels the fanaticism that is at its heart. To say that Al Qaeda is a fringe group may be reassuring, but it is false. Read the Arab press in the aftermath of the attacks and you will detect a not-so-hidden admiration for bin Laden. Or consider this from the Pakistani

newspaper *The Nation*: "September 11 was not mindless terrorism for terrorism's sake. It was reaction and revenge,
even retribution." Why else is America's response to the terror attacks so deeply constrained by fears of an "Islamic
backlash" on the streets? Pakistan will dare not allow Washington the use of its bases. Saudi Arabia trembles at the
thought of having to help us publicly. Egypt pleads that our
strikes be as limited as possible. The problem is not that
Osama bin Laden believes that this is a religious war against
America. It's that millions of people across the Islamic world
seem to agree.

This awkward reality has led some in the West to dust off
old essays and older prejudices predicting a "clash of civilizations" between the West and Islam. The historian Paul
Johnson has argued that Islam is intrinsically an intolerant
and violent religion. Other scholars have disagreed, pointing out that Islam condemns the slaughter of innocents and
prohibits suicide. Nothing will be solved by searching for
"true Islam" or quoting the Qur'an. The Qur'an is a vast,
vague book, filled with poetry and contradictions (much
like the Bible). You can find in it condemnations of war and
incitements to struggle, beautiful expressions of tolerance
and stern strictures against unbelievers. Quotations from it
usually tell us more about the person who selected the pas-
sages than about Islam. Every religion is compatible with
the best and the worst of humankind. Through its long
history, Christianity has supported inquisitions and anti-
Semitism, but also human rights and social welfare.

Searching the history books is also of limited value. From

the Crusades of the eleventh century to the Turkish expansion of the fifteenth century to the colonial era in the early twentieth century, Islam and the West have often battled militarily. This tension has existed for hundreds of years, during which there have been many periods of peace and even harmony. Until the 1950s, for example, Jews and Christians lived peaceably under Muslim rule. In fact, Bernard Lewis, the pre-eminent historian of Islam, has argued that for much of history religious minorities did better under Muslim rulers than they did under Christian ones. All that has changed in the past few decades. So surely the relevant question we must ask is, Why are we in a particularly difficult phase right now? What has gone wrong in the world of Islam that explains not the conquest of Constantinople in 1453 or the siege of Vienna of 1683 but September 11, 2001?

Let us first peer inside that vast Islamic world. Many of the largest Muslim countries in the world show little of this anti-American rage. The biggest, Indonesia, had, until the recent Asian economic crisis, been diligently following Washington's advice on economics, with impressive results. The second and third most populous Muslim countries, Pakistan and Bangladesh, have mixed Islam and modernity with some success. While both countries are impoverished, both have voted a woman into power as prime minister, before most Western countries have done so. Next is Turkey, the sixth largest Muslim country in the world, a flawed but functioning secular democracy and a close ally of the West (being a member of NATO).

Only when you get to the Middle East do you see in lurid colors all the dysfunctions that people conjure up when they think of Islam today. In Iran, Egypt, Syria, Iraq, Jordan, the occupied territories, and the Persian Gulf, the resurgence of Islamic fundamentalism is virulent, and a raw anti-Americanism seems to be everywhere. This is the land of suicide bombers, flag-burners, and fiery *mullahs*. As we strike Afghanistan it is worth remembering that not a single Afghan has been tied to a terrorist attack against the United States. Afghanistan is the campground from which an Arab army is battling America.

But even the Arab rage at America is relatively recent. In the 1950s and 1960s it seemed unimaginable that the United States and the Arab world would end up locked in a cultural clash. Egypt's most powerful journalist, Mohamed Heikal, described the mood at the time: "The whole picture of the United States . . . was a glamorous one. Britain and France were fading, hated empires. The Soviet Union was 5,000 miles away and the ideology of communism was anathema to the Muslim religion. But America had emerged from World War II richer, more powerful and more appealing than ever." I first traveled to the Middle East in the early 1970s, and even then the image of America was of a glistening, approachable modernity: fast cars, Hilton hotels, and Coca-Cola. Something happened in these lands. To understand the roots of anti-American rage in the Middle East, we need to plumb not the past three hundred years of history but the past thirty.

The Rulers

IT IS DIFFICULT to conjure up the excitement in the Arab world in the late 1950s as Gamal Abdel Nasser consolidated power in Egypt. For decades Arabs had been ruled by colonial governors and decadent kings. Now they were achieving their dreams of independence, and Nasser was their new savior, a modern man for the postwar era. He was born under British rule, in Alexandria, a cosmopolitan city that was more Mediterranean than Arab. His formative years were spent in the army, the most Westernized segment of the society. With his tailored suits and fashionable dark glasses, he cut an energetic figure on the world stage. "The Lion of Egypt," he spoke for all the Arab world.

Nasser believed that Arab politics needed to be fired by modern ideas like self-determination, socialism, and Arab unity. And before oil money turned the gulf states into golden geese, Egypt was the undisputed leader of the Middle East. So Nasser's vision became the region's. Every regime, from the Baathists in Syria and Iraq to the conservative monarchies of the gulf, spoke in similar terms and tones. It wasn't that they were just aping Nasser. The Middle East desperately wanted to become modern.

It failed. For all their energy these regimes chose bad ideas and implemented them in worse ways. Socialism produced bureaucracy and stagnation. Rather than adjusting to the failures of central planning, the economies never really moved on. The republics calcified into dictatorships. Third World "nonalignment" became pro-Soviet propaganda.

Arab unity cracked and crumbled as countries discovered their own national interests and opportunities. Worst of all, Israel humiliated the Arabs in the wars of 1967 and 1973. When Saddam Hussein invaded Kuwait in 1990, he destroyed the last remnants of the Arab idea.

Look at Egypt today. The promise of Nasserism has turned into a quiet nightmare. The government is efficient in only one area: squashing dissent and strangling civil society. In the past thirty years Egypt's economy has sputtered along while its population has doubled. Unemployment is at 25 percent, and 90 percent of those searching for jobs hold college diplomas. Once the heart of Arab intellectual life, the country produces just 375 books every year (compared with Israel's four thousand). For all the angry protests to foreigners, Egyptians know all this.

Shockingly, Egypt has fared better than its Arab neighbors. Syria has become one of the world's most oppressive police states, a country where twenty-five thousand people can be rounded up and killed by the regime with no consequences. (This in a land whose capital, Damascus, is the oldest continuously inhabited city in the world.) In thirty years Iraq has gone from being among the most modern and secular of Arab countries — with women working, artists thriving, journalists writing — into a squalid playpen for Saddam Hussein's megalomania. Lebanon, a diverse, cosmopolitan society with a capital, Beirut, that was once called the Paris of the East, has become a hellhole of war and terror. In an almost unthinkable reversal of a global pattern, almost every Arab country today is less free than it was thirty years ago. There are few countries in the world of which one can say that.

We think of Africa's dictators as rapacious, but those in the Middle East can be just as greedy. And when contrasted with the success of Israel, Arab failures are even more humiliating. For all its flaws, out of the same desert Israel has created a functioning democracy, a modern society with an increasingly high-technology economy and thriving artistic and cultural life. Israel now has a per capita GDP that equals that of many Western countries.

If poverty produced failure in most of Arabia, wealth produced failure in the rest of it. The rise of oil power in the 1970s gave a second wind to Arab hopes. Where Nasserism failed, petroleum would succeed. But it didn't. All that the rise of oil prices has done over three decades is to produce a new class of rich, superficially Western gulf Arabs, who travel the globe in luxury and are despised by the rest of the Arab world. Look at any cartoons of gulf sheiks in Egyptian, Jordanian, or Syrian newspapers. They are portrayed in the most insulting, almost racist manner: as corpulent, corrupt, and weak. Most Americans think that Arabs should be grateful for our role in the Gulf War, for we saved Kuwait and Saudi Arabia. Most Arabs think that we saved the Kuwaiti and Saudi *royal families*. Big difference.

The money that the gulf sheiks have frittered away is on a scale that is almost impossible to believe. Just one example: A favored prince of Saudi Arabia, at the age of twenty-five, built a palace in Riyadh for $300 million and, as an additional bounty, was given a $1 billion commission on the kingdom's telephone contract with AT&T. Far from producing political progress, wealth has actually had some negative effects. It has enriched and empowered the gulf governments so that, like their Arab brethren, they, too, have become more repressive over time. The Bedouin societies they once ruled have become gilded cages, filled with frustrated, bitter, and discontented young men — some of whom now live in Afghanistan and work with Osama bin Laden. (Bin Laden and some of his aides come from privileged backgrounds in Saudi Arabia.)

By the late 1980s, while the rest of the world was watching old regimes from Moscow to Prague to Seoul to Johannesburg crack, the Arabs were stuck with their aging dictators and corrupt kings. Regimes that might have seemed promising in the 1960s were now exposed as tired, corrupt kleptocracies, deeply unpopular and thoroughly illegitimate. One has to add that many of them are close American allies.

Failed Ideas

ABOUT A DECADE AGO, in a casual conversation with an elderly Arab intellectual, I expressed my frustration that governments in the Middle East had been unable to liberalize their economies and societies in the way that the East Asians had done. "Look at Singapore, Hong Kong, and Seoul," I said, pointing to their extraordinary economic achievements. The man, a gentle, charming scholar, straightened up and replied sharply, "Look at them. They have simply aped the West. Their cities are cheap copies of Houston and Dallas. That may be all right for fishing villages. But we are heirs to one of the great civilizations of the world. We cannot become slums of the West."

This disillusionment with the West is at the heart of the Arab problem. It makes economic advance impossible and political progress fraught with difficulty. Modernization is now taken to mean, inevitably, uncontrollably, Westernization and, even worse, Americanization. This fear has paralyzed Arab civilization. In some ways the Arab world seems less ready to confront the age of globalization than even Africa, despite the devastation that continent has suffered from AIDS and economic and political dysfunction. At least the Africans want to adapt to the new global economy. The Arab world has not yet taken that first step.

The question is how a region that once yearned for modernity could reject it so dramatically. In the Middle Ages the Arabs studied Aristotle (when he was long forgotten in the West) and invented algebra. In the nineteenth century, when the West set ashore in Arab lands, in the form of Napoleon's conquest of Egypt, the locals were fascinated by this powerful civilization. In fact, as the historian Albert Hourani has documented, the nineteenth century saw European-inspired liberal political and social thought flourish in the Middle East.

The colonial era of the late nineteenth and early twentieth centuries raised hopes of British friendship that were to be disappointed, but still Arab elites remained fascinated with the West. Future kings and generals attended Victoria College in Alexandria, learning the speech and manners of British gentlemen. Many then went on to Oxford, Cambridge, and

Sandhurst — a tradition that is still maintained by Jordan's royal family, though now they go to Hotchkiss or Lawrenceville. After World War I, a new liberal age flickered briefly in the Arab world, as ideas about opening up politics and society gained currency in places like Egypt, Lebanon, Iraq, and Syria. But since they were part of a world of kings and aristocrats, these ideas died with those old regimes. The new ones, however, turned out to be just as Western.

Nasser thought his ideas for Egypt and the Arab world were modern. They were also Western. His "national charter" of 1962 reads as if it were written by left-wing intellectuals in Paris or London. (Like many Third World leaders of the time, Nasser was a devoted reader of France's *Le Monde* and Britain's *New Statesman.*) Even his most passionately held project, Pan-Arabism, was European. It was a version of the nationalism that had united Italy and Germany in the 1870s — that those who spoke one language should be one nation.

America thinks of modernity as all good — and it has been almost all good for America. But for the Arab world, modernity has been one failure after another. Each path followed — socialism, secularism, nationalism — has turned into a dead end. While other countries adjusted to their failures, Arab regimes got stuck in their ways. And those that reformed economically could not bring themselves to ease up politically. The Shah of Iran, the Middle Eastern ruler who tried to move his country into the modern era fastest, reaped the most violent reaction in the Iranian revolution of 1979. But even the shah's modernization — compared, for example, with the East Asian approach of hard work, investment, and thrift —

was an attempt to buy modernization with oil wealth.

It turns out that modernization takes more than strongmen and oil money. Importing foreign stuff — Cadillacs, Gulf-streams, and McDonald's — is easy. Importing the inner stuffings of modern society — a free market, political parties, accountability, and the rule of law — is difficult and danger-ous. The gulf states, for example, have gotten modernization lite, with the goods and even the workers imported from abroad. Nothing was homegrown; nothing is even now. As for politics, the gulf governments offered their people a bar-gain: We will bribe you with wealth, but in return let us stay in power. It was the inverse slogan of the American revolu-tion — no taxation, but no representation either.

The new age of globalization has hit the Arab world in a very strange way. Its societies are open enough to be dis-rupted by modernity, but not so open that they can ride the wave. They see the television shows, the fast foods, and the fizzy drinks. But they don't see genuine liberalization in the society, with increased opportunities and greater openness. Globalization in the Arab world is the critic's caricature of globalization — a slew of Western products and billboards with little else. For some in their societies it means more things to buy. For the regimes it is an unsettling, dangerous phenomenon. As a result, the people they rule can look at globalization but for the most part not touch it.

America stands at the center of this world of globalization. It seems unstoppable. If you close the borders, America comes in through the mail. If you censor the mail, it appears in the fast food and faded jeans. If you ban the products, it seeps in through satellite television. Americans are so comfortable with global capitalism and consumer culture that we cannot fathom just how revolutionary these forces are.

Disoriented young men, with one foot in the old world and another in the new, now look for a purer, simpler alternative. Fundamentalism searches for such people everywhere; it, too, has been globalized. One can now find men in Indonesia who regard the Palestinian cause as their own. (Twenty years ago an Indonesian Muslim would barely have known where Palestine was.) Often they learned about this path away from the West while they were in the West. As did Mohamed Atta, the Hamburg-educated engineer who drove the first plane into the World Trade Center.

The Arab world has a problem with its Attas in more than one sense. Globalization has caught it at a bad demographic moment. Arab societies are going through a massive youth bulge, with more than half of most countries' populations under the age of twenty-five. Young men, often better educated than their parents, leave their traditional villages to find work. They arrive in noisy, crowded cities like Cairo, Beirut, and Damascus or go to work in the oil states. (Almost 10 percent of Egypt's working population worked in the gulf at one point.) In their new world they see great disparities of wealth and the disorienting effects of modernity; most unsettlingly, they see women, unveiled and in public places, taking buses, eating in cafés, and working alongside them.

A huge influx of restless young men in any country is bad news. When accompanied by even small economic and social change, it usually produces a new politics of protest. In the past, societies in these circumstances have fallen prey to a search for revolutionary solutions. (France went through a youth bulge just before the French Revolution, as did Iran before its 1979 revolution.) In the case of the Arab world, this revolution has taken the form of an Islamic resurgence.

Enter Religion

NASSER WAS A reasonably devout Muslim, but he had no interest in mixing religion with politics. It struck him as moving backward. This became apparent to the small Islamic parties that supported Nasser's rise to power. The most important one, the Muslim Brotherhood, began opposing him vigorously, often violently. Nasser cracked down on it in 1954, imprisoning more than a thousand of its leaders and executing six. One of those jailed, Sayyid Qutub, a frail man with a fiery pen, wrote a book in prison called *Signposts on the Road*, which in some ways marks the beginnings of modern political Islam or what is often called "Islamic fundamentalism."

In his book, Qutub condemned Nasser as an impious Muslim and his regime as un-Islamic. Indeed, he went on, almost every modern Arab regime was similarly flawed. Qutub envisioned a better, more virtuous polity that was based on strict Islamic principles, a core goal of orthodox Muslims since the 1880s. As the regimes of the Middle East grew more distant and oppressive and hollow in the decades following Nasser, fundamentalism's appeal grew. It flourished because the

Muslim Brotherhood and organizations like it at least tried to give people a sense of meaning and purpose in a changing world, something no leader in the Middle East tried to do.

In his seminal work, *The Arab Predicament*, Fouad Ajami explains, "The fundamentalist call has resonance because it invited men to participate . . . [in] contrast to a political culture that reduces citizens to spectators and asks them to leave things to their rulers. At a time when the future is uncertain, it connects them to a tradition that reduces bewilderment." Fundamentalism gave Arabs who were dissatisfied with their lot a powerful language of opposition.

On that score, Islam had little competition. The Arab world is a political desert with no real political parties, no free press, few pathways for dissent. As a result, the mosque turned into the place to discuss politics. And fundamentalist organizations have done more than talk. From the Muslim Brotherhood to Hamas to Hizbullah, they actively provide social services, medical assistance, counseling, and temporary housing. For those who treasure civil society, it is disturbing to see that in the Middle East these illiberal groups are civil society.

I asked Sheri Berman, a scholar at Princeton who studies the rise of fascist parties in Europe, whether she saw any parallels. "Fascists were often very effective at providing social services," she pointed out. "When the state or political parties fail to provide a sense of legitimacy or purpose or basic services, other organizations have often been able to step into the void. In Islamic countries there is a ready-made source of legitimacy in the religion. So it's not surprising that this is the foundation on which these groups have flourished. The particular form — Islamic fundamentalism — is specific to this region, but the basic dynamic is similar to the rise of Nazism, fascism, and even populism in the United States."

Islamic fundamentalism got a tremendous boost in 1979 when Ayatollah Ruhollah Khomeini toppled the Shah of Iran. The Iranian revolution demonstrated that a powerful ruler could be taken on by groups within society. It also revealed how in a broken society even seemingly benign forces of progress — education and technology — can add to the turmoil. Until the 1970s most Muslims in the Middle East were illiterate and lived in villages and towns. They practiced a kind of street-Islam that had adapted itself to the local culture. Pluralistic and tolerant, these people often worshiped saints, went to shrines, sang religious hymns, and cherished religious art, all technically disallowed in Islam. (This was particularly true in Iran.) By the 1970s, however, people had begun moving out of the villages and their religious experience was not rooted in a specific place. At the same time they were learning to read and they discovered that a new Islam was being preached by the fundamentalists, an abstract faith not rooted in historical experience but literal, puritanical, and by the book. It was Islam of the High Church as opposed to Islam of the village fair.

In Iran, Ayatollah Khomeini used a powerful technology — the audiocassette. His sermons were distributed throughout the country and became the vehicle of opposition to the Shah's repressive regime. But Khomeini was not alone in using the language of Islam as a political tool. Intellectuals, disillusioned by the half-baked or overrapid modernization that was throwing their world into turmoil, were writing books against "Westoxification" and calling the modern Iranian man — half Western, half Eastern — rootless. Fashionable intellectuals, often writing from the comfort of London or Paris, would critique American secularism and consumerism and endorse an Islamic alternative. As theories like these spread across the Arab world, they appealed not to the poorest of the poor, for whom Westernization was magical (it meant food and medicine). They appealed to the half-educated hordes entering the cities of the Middle East or seeking education and jobs in the West.

The fact that Islam is a highly egalitarian religion for the most part has also proved an empowering call for people who felt powerless. At the same time it means that no Muslim really has the authority to question whether someone who claims to be a proper Muslim is one. The fundamentalists, from Sayyid Qutub on, have jumped into that the void. They ask whether people are "good Muslims." It is a question that has terrified the Muslim world. And here we come to the failure not simply of governments but of intellectual and social elites. Moderate Muslims are loath to criticize or debunk the fanaticism of the fundamentalists. Like the moderates in Northern Ireland, they are scared of what would happen to them if they speak their mind.

The biggest Devil's bargain has been made by the moderate monarchies of the Persian Gulf, particularly Saudi Arabia. The Saudi regime has played a dangerous game. It deflects attention from its shoddy record at home by funding religious schools (*madrasahs*) and centers that spread a rigid, puritanical brand of Islam — Wahhabism. In the past thirty years Saudi-funded schools have churned out tens of thousands of half-educated, fanatical Muslims who view the modern world and non-Muslims with great suspicion. America in this worldview is almost always evil.

This exported fundamentalism has in turn infected not just other Arab societies but countries outside the Arab world, like Pakistan. During the eleven-year reign of General Zia ul-Haq, the dictator decided that as he squashed political dissent he needed allies. He found them in the fundamentalists. With the aid of Saudi financiers and functionaries, he set up scores of *madrasahs* throughout the country. They bought him temporary legitimacy but have eroded the social fabric of Pakistan.

If there is one great cause of the rise of Islamic fundamentalism, it is the total failure of political institutions in the Arab world. Muslim elites have averted their eyes from this reality. Conferences at Islamic centers would still rather discuss "Islam and the Environment" than examine the dysfunctions of the current regimes. But as the moderate majority looks the other way, Islam is being taken over by a small poisonous element, people who advocate cruel attitudes toward women, education, the economy, and modern life in general. I have seen this happen in India, where I grew up. The rich, colorful, pluralistic, and easygoing Islam of my youth has turned into a dour, puritanical faith, policed by petty theocrats and religious commissars. The next section deals with what the United States can do to help the Islamic world. But if Muslims do not take it upon themselves to stop their religion from falling prey to medievalists, nothing any outsider can do will save them.

What To Do

IF ALMOST ANY ARAB were to have read this essay so far, he would have objected vigorously by now. "It is all very well to talk about the failures of the Arab world," he would say, "but what about the failures of the West? You speak of long-term decline, but our problems are with specific, cruel American policies." For most Arabs, relations with the United States have been filled with disappointment.

While the Arab world has long felt betrayed by Europe's colonial powers, its disillusionment with America begins most importantly with the creation of Israel in 1948. As the Arabs see it, at a time when colonies were winning independence from the West, here was a state largely composed of foreign people being imposed on a region with Western backing. The anger deepened in the wake of America's support for Israel during the wars of 1967 and 1973, and ever since in its relations with the Palestinians. The daily exposure to Israel's iron-fisted rule over the occupied territories has turned this into the great cause of the Arab — and indeed the broader Islamic — world. Elsewhere, they look at American policy in the region as cynically geared to America's oil interests, supporting thugs and tyrants without any hesitation. Finally, the bombing and isolation of Iraq have become fodder for daily attacks on the United States. While many in the Arab world do not like Saddam Hussein, they believe that the United States has chosen a particularly inhuman method of fighting him — a method that is starving an entire nation.

There is substance to some of these charges, and certainly from the point of view of an Arab, American actions are never going to seem entirely fair. Like any country, America has its interests. In my view, America's greatest sins toward the Arab world are sins of omission. We have neglected to press any regime there to open up its society. This neglect turned deadly in the case of Afghanistan. Walking away from that fractured country after 1989 resulted in the rise of bin Laden and the Taliban. This is not the gravest error a great power can make, but it is a common American one. As F. Scott Fitzgerald explained of his characters in *The Great Gatsby*, "They were careless people, Tom and Daisy — they smashed things up and creatures and then retreated back into their money, or their vast carelessness . . . and let other people clean up the mess." America has not been venal in the Arab world. But it has been careless.

Yet carelessness is not enough to explain Arab rage. After all, if concern for the Palestinians is at the heart of the problem, why have their Arab brethren done nothing for them? (They cannot resettle in any Arab nation but Jordan, and the aid they receive from the gulf states is minuscule.) Israel treats its 1 million Arabs as second-class citizens, a disgrace on its democracy. And yet the tragedy of the Arab world is that Israel accords them more political rights and dignities than most Arab nations give to their own people. Why is the focus of Arab anger on Israel and not those regimes?

The disproportionate feelings of grievance directed at America have to be placed in the overall context of the sense of humiliation, decline, and despair that sweeps the Arab world. After all, the Chinese vigorously disagree with most of America's foreign policy and have fought wars with U.S. proxies. African states feel the same sense of disappointment and unfairness. But they do not work it into a rage against America. Arabs, however, feel that they are under siege from the modern world and that the United States symbolizes this world. Thus every action America takes gets magnified a thousandfold. And even when we do not act, the rumors of our gigantic powers and nefarious deeds still spread. Most Americans would not believe how common the rumor is throughout the Arab world that either the CIA or Israel's Mossad blew up the World Trade Center to justify attacks on Arabs and Muslims. This is the culture from which the suicide bombers have come.

America must now devise a strategy to deal with this form of religious terrorism. As is now widely understood, this will be a long war, with many fronts and battles small and large. Our strategy must be divided along three lines: military, political, and cultural. On the military front — by which I mean war, covert operations, and other forms of coercion — the goal is simple: the total destruction of Al Qaeda. Even if we never understand all the causes of apocalyptic terror, we must do battle against it. Every person who plans and helps in a terrorist operation must understand that he will be tracked and punished. Their operations will be disrupted, their finances drained, their hideouts destroyed. There will be associated costs to pursuing such a strategy, but they will all fade if we succeed. Nothing else matters on the military front.

The political strategy is more complex and more ambitious. At the broadest level, we now have a chance to reorder the international system around this pressing new danger. The degree of cooperation from around the world has been unprecedented. We should not look on this trend suspiciously. Most governments feel threatened by the rise of subnational forces like Al Qaeda. Even some that have clearly supported terrorism in the past, like Iran, seem interested in re-entering the world community and reforming their ways.

We can define a strategy for the post-cold-war era that addresses America's principal national-security need and yet is sustained by a broad international consensus. To do this we will have to give up some cold-war reflexes, such as an allergy to multilateralism, and stop insisting that China is about to rival us militarily or that Russia is likely to re-emerge as a new military threat. (For ten years now, our defense forces have been aligned for everything but the real danger we face. This will inevitably change.)

The purpose of an international coalition is practical and strategic. Given the nature of this war, we will need the constant cooperation of other governments — to make arrests, shut down safe houses, close bank accounts, and share intelligence. Alliance politics has become a matter of high national security. But there is a broader imperative. The United States dominates the world in a way that inevitably arouses envy or anger or opposition. That comes with the power, but we still need to get things done. If we can mask our power in — sorry, work with — institutions like the United Nations Security Council, U.S. might will be easier for much of the world to bear. Bush's father understood this, which is why he ensured that the United Nations sanctioned the Gulf War. The point here is to succeed, and international legitimacy can help us do that.

Now we get to Israel. It is obviously one of the central and most charged problems in the region. But it is a problem to which we cannot offer the Arab world support for its solution — the extinction of the state. We cannot in any way weaken our commitment to the existence and health of Israel. Similarly, we cannot abandon our policy of containing Saddam Hussein. He is building weapons of mass destruction.

However, we should not pursue mistaken policies simply out of spite. Our policy toward Saddam is broken. We have no inspectors in Iraq, the sanctions are — for whatever reason — starving Iraqis and he continues to build chemical and biological weapons. There is a way to reorient our policy to focus our pressure on Saddam and not his people, contain him militarily but not harm common Iraqis economically. Colin Powell has been trying to do this; he should be given leeway to try again. In time we will have to address the broader question of what to do about Saddam, a question that, unfortunately, does not have an easy answer. (Occupying Iraq, even if we could do it, does not seem a good idea in this climate.)

On Israel we should make a clear distinction between its right to exist and its occupation of the West Bank and Gaza.

On the first we should be as unyielding as ever; on the second we should continue trying to construct a final deal along the lines that Bill Clinton and Ehud Barak outlined. I suggest that we do this less because it will lower the temperature in the Arab world — who knows if it will? — than because it's the right thing to do. Israel cannot remain a democracy and continue to occupy and militarily rule 3 million people against their wishes. It's bad for Israel, bad for the Palestinians, and bad for the United States.

But policy changes, large or small, are not at the heart of the struggle we face. The third, vital component to this battle is a cultural strategy. The United States must help Islam enter the modern world. It sounds like an impossible challenge, and it certainly is not one we would have chosen. But America — indeed the whole world — faces a dire security threat that will not be resolved unless we can stop the political, economic, and cultural collapse that lies at the roots of Arab rage. During the cold war the West employed myriad ideological strategies to discredit the appeal of communism, make democracy seem attractive, and promote open societies. We will have to do something on that scale to win this cultural struggle.

First, we have to help moderate Arab states, but on the condition that they embrace moderation. For too long regimes like Saudi Arabia's have engaged in a deadly dance with religious extremism. Even Egypt, which has always denounced fundamentalism, allows its controlled media to rant crazily about America and Israel. (That way they don't rant about the dictatorship they live under.) But more broadly, we must persuade Arab moderates to make the case to their people that Islam is compatible with modern society, that it does allow women to work, that it encourages education and that it has welcomed people of other faiths and creeds. Some of this they will do — September 11 has been a wake-up call for many. The Saudi regime denounced and broke its ties to the Taliban (a regime that it used to glorify as representing pure Islam). The Egyptian press is now making the case for military action. The United States and the West should do their own work as well. We can fund moderate Muslim groups and scholars and broadcast fresh thinking across the Arab world, all aimed at breaking the power of the fundamentalists.

Obviously we will have to help construct a new political order in Afghanistan after we have deposed the Taliban regime. But beyond that we have to press the nations of the Arab world — and others, like Pakistan, where the virus of fundamentalism has spread — to reform, open up, and gain legitimacy. We need to do business with these regimes; yet, just as we did with South Korea and Taiwan during the cold war, we can ally with these dictatorships and still push them toward reform. For those who argue that we should not engage in nation-building, I would say foreign policy is not theology. I have myself been skeptical of nation-building in places where our interests were unclear and it seemed unlikely that we would stay the course. In this case, stable political development is the key to reducing our single greatest security threat. We have no option but to get back into the nation-building business.

It sounds like a daunting challenge, but there are many good signs. Al Qaeda is not more powerful than the combined force of many determined governments. The world is indeed uniting around American leadership, and perhaps we will see the emergence, for a while, of a new global community and consensus, which could bring progress in many other areas of international life. Perhaps most important, Islamic fundamentalism still does not speak to the majority of the Muslim people. In Pakistan, fundamentalist parties have yet to get more than 10 percent of the vote. In Iran, having experienced the brutal puritanism of the *mullahs*, people are yearning for normalcy. In Egypt, for all the repression, the fundamentalists are a potent force but so far not dominant. If the West can help Islam enter modernity in dignity and peace, it will have done more than achieved security. It will have changed the world.

Acknowledgments

We gratefully acknowledge all those who gave permission for written material to appear in this book. We have made every effort to trace and contact copyright holders. If an error or omission is brought to our notice we will be pleased to remedy the situation in future editions of this book. For further information, please contact the publisher.

Excerpt from *The World's Religions* by Huston Smith. Copyright © 1991 by Huston Smith. Reprinted by permission of HarperCollins Publishers, Inc.

Excerpt from *Islam Today* by Akbar S. Ahmed. Copyright © 2001 by Akbar Ahmed. Reprinted by permission of I.B. Tauris Publishers, London.

Excerpt from *The Essential Koran* by Thomas Cleary. Copyright © 1994 by Thomas Cleary. Reprinted by permission of HarperCollins Publishers, Inc.

Excerpt from *One Thousand Roads to Mecca* by Michael Wolfe. Copyright © 1997 by Michael Wolfe. Used by permission of Grove/Atlantic, Inc.

"Home is Here" by Mark Singer. Copyright © 2001 by Mark Singer. Originally appeared in the *New Yorker*, October 15, 2001. Reprinted by permission of the author.

Excerpt from *Shah of Shahs* by Ryszard Kapuściński. Copyright © 1982 by Ryszard Kapuściński. Reprinted by permission of Harcourt Brace.

Excerpt from *Among the Believers* by V. S. Naipaul. Copyright © 1982 by V. S. Naipaul. Used by permission of Random House, Inc.

About the Editors

John Miller and Aaron Kenedi run Miller Design Partners and are the editors of more than fifty art and literary books including *God's Breath: Sacred Scriptures of the World* — praised by *Publishers Weekly* as "an essential companion for students of world religions."